The Success Myth

The Success Myth

How to Have it All and Still be Happy

CAROL GUILD

Published by Motivational Press, Inc.
2360 Corporate Circle
Suite 400
Henderson, NV 89074
www.MotivationalPress.com

www.carolguild.com

Manufactured in the United States of America.

ISBN: 978-1-935723-98-1

CONTENTS

Dedication

To Dan:
Who keeps love, laughter, and happiness in my life.
You have changed everything for me.

Acknowledgements

Because this book draws on personal and professional experiences throughout my life, while writing it I often reflected on who most influenced me. My professional life was influenced by three people. My father, Wayne Goodling, was a self-made businessman who taught me about business as I "helped" him throughout my childhood and teen years. He taught me many other lessons as well about helping others and that happiness begins within you. My older brother once said to me, "You are your father's daughter." It was a wonderful compliment. My mentor, Bob Miner, hired me fresh out of college and turned me into a successful marketer by unselfishly teaching me everything he could about the world of advertising, publishing, and marketing. And Mike Peck, who I worked with for many years, exemplifies all the attributes a great business owner should have. Without Mike I would never have owned my own business.

On the personal side there are three people whose influence has stayed with me. My mother, Ruth Dressler Goodling, was absent from much of my childhood but she always told me I could be anything I wanted and encouraged me to pursue my dreams. My grandmother, Mary Goodling, was the constant role model in my life, both before and after my parents divorced in 1960. My older brother, Rob Goodling, generously shared his amazing creative spirit and love of everything cultural and artistic with his kid sister. We weathered many tumultuous years while growing up, but he made them fun and exciting. Although our younger brother, Randy, was separated from us as an infant, today the three of us enjoy an unbreakable bond of love and respect that I believe is rare.

In my journey to get this book published I have met many other aspiring writers, hundreds of successful people, and many who have helped me through the journey. No one is more significant, however, than my wonderful author's coach, Ann McIndoo. Her wisdom, cheerfulness, guidance, and support kept me motivated and helped me learn all that I didn't know. Without her this book would most likely still be in my head.

I dedicated this book to my better half, Dan Guild. How lucky I've been to find a soul mate who nurtures my dreams and lets me into his. With him it is so easy to create new dreams that are ours. Without him my life would not be as wonderful as it is.

Introduction

My Personal Success Myth

"If it's good, it's wonderful. If it's bad, it's experience."
Victoria Holt

In 1968 I graduated from my high school in a small, rural Central Pennsylvania town. There were only 74 kids in my class.

In the section of our high school yearbook that profiled the seniors, we each had to put our ambition for after graduation. Mine was, "To be successful."

At the time I had no idea how vague that ambition was. Most of my classmates were much more specific. They wanted to be teachers, accountants, nurses, or engineers. One wanted to become a millionaire. Another wanted to travel around the world. And there was one who had no ambition.

My best friend's ambition was to get married. She did it three times.

From this small class in a rural high school there were as many different views of what success would be as there were students.

At that time I had a dream of what I wanted to do. Unlike my best friend, I didn't want to get married. I wanted to go to college, major in journalism, and get a job with a leading newspaper or news service. I wanted to travel around the world to report on exciting stories. I planned to publish my first novel at the age of 40.

Instead, at the age of 40 I had worked for 17 years in advertising and marketing. By the age of 45 I owned an advertising & marketing agency. I was married for the second time and had a teenage son.

By the age of 55 my son had graduated from college and was out on his own. My husband and I were living in a beautiful home in an elegant "old money" neighborhood in my community. My parents were still living. I had a close circle of good friends, a bigger circle of professional friends, and my best friend from high school was still my best friend.

I volunteered for my favorite organizations and causes, was active in several civic groups, and enjoyed public recognition for my marketing expertise as a speaker and workshop presenter at dinners and conferences.

By all outward appearances I had an ideal life.

But I was dreadfully unhappy. Despite having so much that appeared to be positive, my life was actually full of obligations, demands, and stress. I worked constantly. My time was being controlled by the needs of others.

This wasn't the life I wanted, and I felt trapped in it.

My business owned me instead of me owning it. My marriage was in a constant state of conflict and unhappiness. I didn't have time to spend with my friends, and wasn't even there for my best friend when her husband passed away. I started to gain weight from the stress, and I wasn't getting any younger.

I had fallen into what I call the complacency trap. It was easier to stay where I was than make a change. But the idea that this would continue to be my life for years to come was bleak and depressing. I decided I had to change it. I had to escape from the trap.

I started to think about how to change it and I created more questions than answers. They were big questions such as:

What did I really want?

What would my ideal life look like?

How could I possibly make the drastic changes that would get me out of the life I had?

What if I made changes and discovered I still didn't have the life I wanted? Then what would I do?

The idea of starting over at the age of 55 was frightening and daunting. There were great risks—especially in my finances and relationships.

Change would bring hope and opportunity. But it also would bring uncertainty and fear.

I started to question if it was just me. What was wrong with me that I had so much and wasn't satisfied?

I began to talk to other people who also appeared to be living a life of success and accomplishment, and what I found was amazing. It wasn't just me. I wasn't alone.

The majority of people I spoke with, who appeared to be immensely successful and to "have it all," were also struggling with how to create the life they really wanted. For some it was just a few small things they wanted to change. Others were like me and wanted to totally change their lives. The one thing everyone had in common was they wanted more control, more time, more happiness, more personal fulfillment, and more freedom in their lives.

Like me, they were living the Success Myth, which is . . . if you've achieved enough wealth, possessions, power, influence, prestige, fame, position, or whatever you thought success meant for you, you would have it all. Instead, despite having it all, we were unhappy.

Statistics show that things don't work out the way we expect on the path to success.

- The typical American changes jobs or careers 3-5 times, constantly looking for something better, different, or more rewarding. Satisfaction from work can be elusive, even at the top of the corporate ladder where seven-figure salaries create wealth but often don't create happiness. People often pursue careers based on pay rates, earning potential, or personal prestige, not on doing something that gives them pleasure every day.

- 50% of first marriages end in divorce. 67% of second marriages end in divorce. The successful relationship is elusive and most of us have difficulty balancing success in other areas with success on a personal level. We are so controlled by the pursuit of success, as defined by money and possessions, that we ignore our relationships or try to squeeze that part of our lives into small spaces of "quality time."

- 59% of Americans have acquired debt they can't pay off instead of acquiring savings or wealth. 67% of college grads start their adult lives with student loan debt of more than $23,000. Many people exhibit the outward appearance of success but actually live on borrowed money. For the young, getting to the point of building success is more challenging than ever before. When prestige and respect are measured by the size of our homes, the number of expensive "toys" we own, the cars we drive, the vacations we take, and the pastimes we indulge in, we will do almost anything to keep the outward illusion of success and affluence.

- 19 million Americans (9.5%) are clinically depressed. 30% of Americans have trouble sleeping. 60% of Americans are overweight. 1 in 3 are considered obese. These figures relate to people across the full spectrum of success. Many highly successful people deal with depression. The stress that often comes with a successful life brings pressures that create health risks. You don't have to think long or hard to start a list of successful people who ended their own lives to escape from the trappings of their success.

Successful people are controlled by their success. It feeds an appetite for more. More wealth. Bigger and better possessions. More influence. More stature. More power. More fame.

Successful people are identified by their success. It is who they are. That's why it can be impossible to step away from it. A step back, a step down, or in a different direction, can be perceived as failure.

When I thought about how to change my life, I didn't want to be perceived as a failure—in anything. Not in my business, my marriage, or any other outward appearances. Eventually I realized that to change, however, I had to teach myself not to care what others thought. I needed to make myself happy. People who truly cared about me, and who were true friends, would still be there, and the ones who wouldn't still be there didn't matter after all.

For months I worked on ways to change my life, but continually became overwhelmed about where to start, what to do first, and how to do it, while keeping my life in some balance during the process.

Finally the light bulb came on. For 33 years I had been successful in marketing. I helped businesses develop and launch new products. I helped them make acquisitions of other companies. I helped them build their brands and grow their sales and profits. I facilitated strategic planning meetings and SWOT analysis for them to identify their strengths, weaknesses, opportunities, and threats.

So I thought, what if I took my experience in branding and strategic planning for products and businesses and applied it to my personal life? What if I looked at "me" as a brand?

Could I take the process I used for developing strategic plans for my clients and adapt it to develop a strategic plan for my life?

The answer was "Yes." So I created a process for creating the life I wanted by developing my personal brand. It took me almost two years to create the process, but at the age of 57 I took the steps to change my life.

It worked. That's why I wrote this book. To show you how to do it too.

The Success Myth helps you understand why the things you thought would bring success and happiness to your life can fail you, and shows you the process for how to have all you want and still be happy.

I am not a financial expert. I am not a psychologist. I am a marketing consultant who has become a personal branding expert. The process I developed uses branding and marketing concepts to change your life into your personal brand.

You'll see how this process helps you determine what you can and should change, and how to go about doing it. My process deals with all the areas in the success myth: money, ambition, relationships, recognition, possessions, time, health, purpose, and self-esteem.

You'll identify what "real" success is for you. You'll have the direction you need to make the simple decisions, confidence to make the difficult ones, and the wisdom to recognize the wrong ones.

In short: You'll discover how to have your success and be in control of it on **your terms**. I know it will work for you, because I did it and it worked for me.

Chapter 1

So, How is Life Treating You?

"Anyone can face a crisis.
It's day to day living that wears you out."

Anton Chekhov

Before you start to develop your personal brand and decide what success means for you, make an assessment of your life.

Most of us are so busy with our day-to-day routines that we forget about living the life we want, and deal with the life we get. A 2011 Gallup survey found that only 47% of us are very satisfied with our lives. Most of us are somewhat satisfied—enough that we don't feel pressured to make big changes, but not enough that we are living the life we want.

In business, one of the ways I rate customer satisfaction is with the Net Promoter Score, a management tool developed by Fred Reichheld that was introduced in the *Harvard Business Review* in 2003. The score is a metric that measures customer loyalty and satisfaction with a business.

I use the same process to help people measure their level of satisfaction with their lives, by answering the questions in my "How is Life Treating You?" quiz.

Respond to the following statements by circling a number 1 through 10 that follows each statement.

A 1 answer is "totally do <u>not</u> agree." A 10 answer is "totally agree." Use the 1 through 10 range to rate your level of agreement.

A 5 is "sometimes agree", with the numbers in between each being a range; such as 2, 3, and 4 are a range that gets your from totally do not agree to sometimes agree, and 6,7,8, and 9 are a range that gets you from sometimes agree to totally agree.

Question 1.

I enjoy my job and look forward to going to work.

1   2   3   4   5   6   7   8   9   10

Question 2.

I am happy in my relationship status with my spouse, significant other, partner, girl friend/boy friend, etc. and wouldn't change anything about our relationship. *[Note: if you are not in a relationship but want to be, then you would indicate you are not happy. If you are not in a relationship and are happy with that status, indicate that you are happy.]*

1   2   3   4   5   6   7   8   9   10

Question 3.

I have all the time I want and need to do things I enjoy. (Hobbies, pastimes, sports, arts, interests.)

1   2   3   4   5   6   7   8   9   10

Question 4.

I have enough money from my earnings to sustain my current lifestyle and get things I need.

1   2   3   4   5   6   7   8   9   10

Question 5.

I have safety nets in place (insurance, savings, investments, etc.) to protect my lifestyle from an accident or catastrophic event.

1   2   3   4   5   6   7   8   9   10

Question 6.

I take care of myself through a healthy diet, exercise, and lifestyle and am in good health.

1   2   3   4   5   6   7   8   9   10

Question 7.

I enjoy being with my immediate family (parents, siblings, children) and look forward to spending time together.

1   2   3   4   5   6   7   8   9   10

Question 8.

I tend to look at all situations with a positive attitude and seldom complain.

1   2   3   4   5   6   7   8   9   10

Question 9.

I have close friends who will be there for me if needed and I will be there for them if needed.

1   2   3   4   5   6   7   8   9   10

Question 10.

I am satisfied with the way I look—my shape, weight, and physical appearance.

1   2   3   4   5   6   7   8   9   10

Question 11.

I cope well with things I can't control so they rarely cause me to feel stress, anger, or frustration.

1   2   3   4   5   6   7   8   9   10

Question 12.

I only buy things I really need and will use and don't spend money for things I don't need and rarely or never use.

1   2   3   4   5   6   7   8   9   10

Question 13.

I have the time and money to support causes I believe in and enjoy being able to help those causes.

1   2   3   4   5   6   7   8   9   10

Question 14.

I regularly participate in ways to bring balance and inner peace to cope with the demands and stress in my life (such as through religion, meditation, enjoying nature, spa treatments, therapeutic massage, and other calming activities.)

1   2   3   4   5   6   7   8   9   10

Question 15.

I enjoy what I do for a living so much, that if I didn't need the money I earn I would continue to do it without getting paid.

1   2   3   4   5   6   7   8   9   10

Question 16.

I am so happy with my life that I never fantasize about changing it.

1   2   3   4   5   6   7   8   9   10

To find out how life is treating you, add the numbers you circled and write the total in this box:

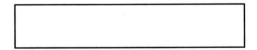

You'll have a possible low total of 16 to a high total of 160 if you answered all the questions. The lower your number the less happy you are with your life. The higher the number the more happy you are.

Here is a guideline of what your total means:

16-32: Totally unhappy and really want to change your life.

33-64: Unhappy with most of your life and want to make many changes.

65-79: Unhappy with many parts of your life and want to change them.

80-96: Satisfied with some things in your life, but want to change other things.

97-127: Satisfied with many things about your life and only want to change some things.

128-144: Satisfied with most of your life and would make only a few changes.

145-160: You are very much in control of your life and very satisfied with it.

To make changes that will have the most impact for you, look at which questions have low numbers and you'll know what areas of life contribute the most to your unhappiness. Look at the questions with high numbers and you'll know what parts of your life are working for you. This will help you focus on the actions needed to take control of your life.

Chapter 2

Put Yourself First

"Success is getting what you want.
Happiness is wanting what you get."

W.P. Kinsella

Congratulations for taking this first step in controlling your success instead of letting it control you. Your total score from the quiz in Chapter 1 tells you what level of satisfaction you have achieved with all areas of your life.

Look at the specific questions and answers for those areas where your numbers were low. They'll help guide you through your process.

In the world of advertising and marketing, I study what people want, and use that knowledge to motivate behavior so my clients can sell their products. I get people to make emotional connections with the brands I promote. Consumers use those brand connections to define themselves through the products they use.

Perhaps nowhere was this process demonstrated more clearly than in the "Get a Mac" Apple ad campaign that ran from 2006 to 2009. In the campaign two actors started each ad by declaring either, "I'm a Mac" or "I'm a PC." It was a masterful campaign that demonstrated just how closely consumers associate themselves with the brands they love.

What I will help you do in this book is see yourself as a brand you love. In taking you through the success myth process, to get you the happiness and life you want, *you must learn to put yourself first.* Each chapter in the book is a sequential step in the process of doing that.

As you read the book you'll see how each new chapter builds on, and relates back to, earlier ones. You'll begin to make the connections of what you want, what you have, what choices you've made that aren't getting you to the life you want, what you can and should change, and how to do it.

The process works for people at any age or stage in life, just as the principles of strategic planning work for all businesses, whether in startup mode, growth phases, or as established leaders in their industries. You can apply the process to your situation.

If you are a young adult, in your 20s or 30s, this book will help you decide what you should do with your life so it's right for you. Don't allow life to control you, take control of it. You're in charge. Plus, you can use this process throughout your life. You'll have a strategic plan to guide you. You'll know how to revise and change that plan in response to opportunities and circumstances you can't foresee now.

If you are in the middle of your adult life, established in your job and career, raising children, and trying to survive all that life has thrown at you, this process will be one of the most liberating, energizing things you have ever done. It will help you balance the demands you deal with every day and develop a plan that gets you back to being in control. It will show you why you must put yourself first, before your family and friends, if you are to be the person you want to be, for yourself and them.

If you are an older adult, your children are grown, or perhaps you've never had children, and have worked all your life to build the success that now controls you and has become your identity, this book lets you know that there is no age that is too old to make the changes you want and create a life you love! You are at an age where you've acquired more trappings of success than those who are younger. But you also have the most immediate ability to free yourself of the trappings and get the most happiness for your life in the years ahead.

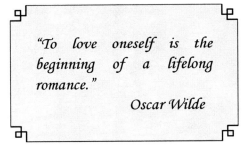

"To love oneself is the beginning of a lifelong romance."

Oscar Wilde

Imagine a life where every day is lived the way you want. Where you've eliminated the major stresses and frustrations you've been dealing with. Where you surround yourself with actions, things, and people that enhance your dreams. Where you have the confidence and power to control your situation. Where you have found the right balance of money and stature for **_your_** vision of yourself, and not to impress others. Where you have the freedom, time, and resources to do what you want, when you want, whether for yourself or to help others.

To do this you <u>must </u>be willing to put yourself first.

That doesn't mean you mistreat, disrespect, or disregard other people in your life.

But when you see yourself as a brand, you quickly realize that you can't do spin-offs of your brand (those things you do for others) unless your core brand is a successful one. If Coke hadn't been a successful soft drink brand, there would be no Diet Coke or Cherry Coke as spin-offs of the original. Like Coke, you must focus on your own brand first. Then you will be in a position to look at how you fit others into your life.

Only when you put yourself in control can you achieve what you want.

Chapter 3

Define Your Personal Brand

"The real challenge isn't to simply survive.
It's to survive as yourself."

Elia Kazan

The movie star we know as Cary Grant was born as Archie Leach. He had a poor, unhappy childhood in Liverpool, England, which he left at the age of 17.

He came to America, and was still known as Archie Leach when he arrived in Hollywood. It was there he developed the persona of Cary Grant as the person he wanted to be; elegant, suave, and sophisticated; yet funny, charming, and self-effacing. "Everyone wants to be Cary Grant. I want to be Cary Grant," is a statement he made in an interview. Grant imagined the person he wanted to be and he became that person.

Archie Leach became the brand we know as Cary Grant.

Knowing what type of person you want to be, appreciating and accepting those things that make you unique, and deciding how you want to be perceived by others, are the essential steps in creating the self-esteem and self-perception that defines your personal brand.

You will never have complete happiness in your life if you don't make your own happiness a top priority. It starts within you. Ask yourself this question: "Am I the person I want to be?"

When you don't put yourself first you turn control of your life over to others. When others control your life you begin to feel used, unappreciated, and taken for granted. You may feel that people don't care about you; they only care about what you can do for them. You become almost invisible if you put your dreams and desires aside to accommodate others.

Putting yourself first is crucial to defining your personal brand.

In defining your brand you must first look at your strengths.

What do you like about yourself? What things do you do just for your own satisfaction and well-being? Are you allowing your strengths to work for you or do you hide them? What are the things you do that cause others to notice you and compliment you? Do others listen to you when you speak showing that they value what you say and think?

Are you ignoring opportunities because you aren't putting yourself first? Have you declined, refused, and walked away from offers, invitations, requests, and possibilities because you prioritized the needs and wants of others more than your own?

Compare yourself to an actual product brand. Coke is the leading product brand in soft drinks. However, if Coke failed to take advantage of market opportunities because it wouldn't be fair to Pepsi, they would no longer be the top brand. It's ridiculous to even think they would do that.

Yet people do it all the time. People fail to take advantage of opportunities because it would cause disruption to the other people in their lives. Thinking of yourself as a brand allows you to keep yourself on top.

When Archie Leach created Cary Grant he decided what he wanted Cary Grant to be. He focused on attributes such as being debonair, sophisticated, and dashing. He defined the person he wanted to be and he became that person.

He is still considered to be one of Hollywood's most definitive leading men. The American Film Institute named him the second greatest male star of all time, second only to Humphrey Bogart. Of all the roles he played, he said he considered playing Cary Grant to be his best.

Now it's time for you to create your brand.

List all the things that DESCRIBE who YOU are.

_____

_____

_____

_____

_____

_____

_____

_____

_____

_____

_____

_____

_____

_____

The Blogger RJ Walters lists his brand attributes on his home page at RJs Corner (rjscorner.net) under the heading "About Me." He lets you know that he is a Will Rogers fan, a retired furniture maker, a frequent vacationer, a husband, and a guy with unique views of life. These are just a few of his brand attributes. He has 22 on his list.

Look at your list. These are your brand attributes. Now that you've defined them, decide if there are other attributes you want associated with your brand. Is there anything you want to change?

In the world of advertising, brands are changed all the time. Think of how many products are advertised as "new and improved." Reinventing yourself is part of the branding process.

Is there anything about yourself, or your life, you don't like? If yes, change it. Will creating the life you want require you to reinvent yourself as the new and improved you? If yes, it's never too late to do that. High profile people do it all the time.

Actors such as Robert Downey, Jr., politicians such as Bill Clinton, sports stars such as Michael Vick, and musicians such as P. Diddy, are all people who changed their brands to replace negative perceptions with positive ones.

List all the things you would like to CHANGE about YOURSELF.

_____

_____

_____

_____

_____

_____

_____

_____

_____

_____

_____

_____

_____

_____

> *"I thought, I need to reinvent myself. I want every day of life to be wonderful, fascinating, interesting, and creative. And what am I going to do to make that happen?"*
>
> *Karen Allen*

The combination of your two lists describes the brand you are today and the brand you want to become. Seeing your future potential is something you've been doing since childhood, when adults would ask what you wanted to be when you grew up. You probably had a childhood dream, or perhaps several different dreams, that you never turned into reality.

Taking control of your brand, putting yourself first, and creating the life you want lets you turn your dreams into reality.

When you apply successful business strategies to your personal life you begin to see things differently. When a business is sold, the value of the sale isn't just the products and physical assets that are the tangible part of the business. The value is in the brand.

Coca Cola is the most valuable brand in the world. It has an estimated brand value of $77.8 billion, yet its annual gross income is just $26.8 billion—much less than the value of the brand.

Elizabeth Taylor is a valuable Hollywood brand. She died in 2011 but in 2012 she generated $210 million in sales. She is the highest earning deceased celebrity, surpassing Michael Jackson, Elvis, and Marilyn Monroe. That's brand value!

Of course everyday people aren't celebrity brands. But the same concept that applies to celebrities applies to you. When you develop your personal brand you define success on your terms. You create the life you want. You determine the way you'll touch the lives of others and how others see you.

To create the life you want, to have it all and still be happy, you need to be your biggest fan. As you create the strategic plan for your life you'll know where and how to prioritize each part to achieve what success is for you. Put yourself first, create a positive world for yourself, take the actions needed to be in control of your success, and you'll create a fabulous personal brand.

Chapter 4

Picture Your Ideal Life

"If you don't know where you're going,
you'll wind up somewhere else."

Yogi Bera

In marketing I use the "problem/solution" scenario to develop ad messages. Marketers define a problem then show consumers how their product solves that problem.

Think about all the products and services you buy to solve a problem in your life.

Want to be healthier? The marketplace is full of products that promise results—from exercise equipment to pills to natural and organic foods.

Want to be wealthier? You're bombarded with all kinds of ads about ways to have access to money—from credit cards to investment opportunities, insurance offers, sweepstakes, lotteries, and more.

Want to have that perfect relationship? From dating and matchmaking services to all kinds of personal grooming and enhancement products, advertising presents a variety of options to make yourself attractive so you meet that perfect someone.

The categories of goods and services that solve problems are endless. Marketers know the best way to get consumers to make a purchase is to convince them that all they have to do to have a better life is buy what they're selling. It is simply not true.

As you develop a plan for your life, apply the problem/solution process to yourself and you'll see the best way to achieve a better life is through what you do, not what you buy.

One of the most famous problem solvers in the world didn't work in the field of marketing, he worked in the field of physics. He solved problems no one knew existed. Not only was he a regular Einstein, he was THE Einstein.

As a boy, Albert Einstein did not do well in school. The rigid school structure and teaching methods stifled his creativity. His teachers saw no potential in him. He failed to get respectable grades in most of his classes, including math.

After college he struggled for more than two years to get hired in a teaching position. He finally settled for a job evaluating patent applications as an assistant examiner at the Bern, Switzerland Federal Office for Intellectual Property.

But Einstein never allowed these discouragements to kill his creative ideas. He sought out others who thought like him and shared his interests. He eventually became respected as one of the leading scientists in Bern, and later became one of the most influential physicists in the world, winning the Nobel Prize in physics for pioneering quantum theory.

To apply the problem/solution process for yourself, unleash your creativity and discover the Einstein within you. Your aspirations don't need to be Nobel Prize worthy. They only need to make you happy.

Knowing what you truly want your life to be is an essential first step in using the problem/solution process. Until you can define your ideal life, you can't find the solutions that are right for you.

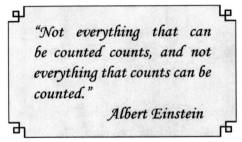

"Not everything that can be counted counts, and not everything that counts can be counted."

Albert Einstein

For Einstein, his ideal life was spending his time questioning the accepted standards of science and mathematics, and tinkering with changing them. It was his passion.

What is the ideal life for you? What are your passions? What is your ambition?

Let's start on your Personal Success Plan.

When I work with businesses on strategic planning, the first thing I ask is for them to tell me what success looks like for them. What do they hope to achieve as a result of the plan we're going to create? The same process will work for you in developing your personal brand. Start the strategic plan for your life with this question: "What does success look like for me?"

Success and happiness are different for each of us. The biggest marketing lie is "one size fits all." That's equally true in life. There is no one plan that works for each of us. There is no magic lamp you can rub to make a genie appear who will give you what you want.

You are the only person who can do that. And you can do it regardless of your age or current financial situation. You just need to start.

When businesses do strategic plans, they are usually for 12 months, 3 years, or 5 years. But they are never "forever." The same will be true of the strategic plan you create for yourself.

Because life is organic, things will happen that you can't foresee today. Some will be opportunities, others will be threats. Some will make you stronger, others may make you weaker.

But, by having a plan, you'll be ready to deal with whatever comes your way. You'll have a framework to evaluate and keep everything in perspective for your big picture because you've identified what success is for you.

Go into this process knowing you will revisit your plan often. I revisit mine every year and modify it as needed.

Start by envisioning your successful outcomes. Describe your ideal life. Do it without thinking about money. There are to be no restrictions on your thinking as you envision your successful outcomes. Think that anything is possible.

Here are some questions to get you started.

What do you want to do with your life? What gives you pleasure? What are you good at?

Where would you like to live?

Do you want to get married? If you are married, do you want to stay married to the person you're with? Do you want children? Or, if you have children, what will you do when they are adults and no longer in your day-to-day world?

What type of career or job would you like to be doing where you look forward to every day? Do you have that job now? If not, how do you get that job?

If you don't want to work, or are retired from work, what do you want to do with your time each day?

> *"The first step to getting the things out of life that you want is this: Decide what you want."*
>
> *Ben Stein*

How important are your friends and extended family? What do you want time to do that you can't do now? What fills you with pure joy and personal satisfaction?

Use these questions as a guideline and write your answers to this:

What would YOU like YOUR life to be?

In the spaces below, create your perfect life. Make a list of those things that define what you would like your life to be. What would you like to do when you get up each day? Envision success for yourself. I recommend you write your answers in pencil, because as you read through *The Success Myth* you are likely to come back and make changes to this list.

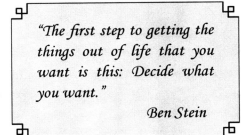

_____

_____

_____

_____

_____

_____

_____

_____

_____

_____

_____

_____

_____

Put a check mark in front of everything on your list that is already happening for you. Then look at those things without a check mark. That's what you need to focus on. These are your goals and ambitions. They define your personal brand.

To take care of your brand means that all of your decisions should get you closer to realizing your goals and ambitions. Most of us share our lives with other people—spouses, partners, and significant others—who have an impact on our brand by influencing the decisions we make. Here's where branding becomes an important indicator for you.

When consumers choose a brand, whether it's a car, cereal, computer, soft drink, or any of thousands of other products, that brand is a reflection of who they are. The same is true with that significant other person in your life. You chose each other because you are brands that each of you wanted. Therefore you should be able to make decisions that get you closer to the life you want. If you discover that the life you want is very different for each of you, that may be a key reason you haven't found what success is for you.

Perhaps your goals and ambitions include wanting to find someone to share your life with. Today the fastest growing type of household in America is the single person household. 28% of households have just one person—the highest rate ever. Many single people want to change that status as part of their ideal life.

For most of us, describing what we want our life to be usually includes having someone to share it with. We need to find our compatible brand, something you'll learn more about in Chapter 10.

The things on your list are like destinations on a map. You are identifying all the "places" you want to go to. Now you're ready to decide how you're going to get there.

Chapter 5

Reclaim Your Dreams

*"Plan for the future because that's where you are going
to spend the rest of your life."*

Mark Twain

When I work on strategic planning with businesses and organizations I have a list called "10 Ways to Kill a Great Idea." These "killer" phrases are things I will not allow to be said during the planning process and they include common comments such as, "We've always done it this way," and, "It's not in the budget."

What are the phrases—the excuses—you've used to kill your great ideas? Eliminate them so you can make your dreams come true.

The excuse, "It's not in the budget," is the one I hear most often when I work with businesses on their strategies. In reality, money, or the lack of it, is never the problem. And it isn't the problem for you. Most dreams don't require immense wealth. But they may require you to prioritize how you manage and spend your money (which is discussed in more detail in Chapter 7.)

What choices have you made in your life to please others? How much control have you given others over decisions that prevent you from realizing your dreams? Do you find yourself doing things you really don't want to do because you feel obligated to live up to another's expectations?

When things like that happen over and over it isn't long until you give up on your dreams. Eventually you can get into a rut where family, friends, and even co-workers determine what you do and how you live. Don't give up control of your dreams. That's why you must put yourself first.

In Chapter 4 you identified what you want your life to be. These are your dreams. Before starting a plan to realize your dreams, you need to face all the reasons they never happened. To do that, write down the answers to this question:

What PREVENTS YOU from having the life you WANT?

_____

_____

_____

_____

_____

_____

_____

_____

_____

_____

_____

_____

_____

_____

This list shows you what the "killer phrases" have been for your life. To move forward in realizing your dreams I want you to ask yourself "Why did this happen" in response to each item you listed.

Common things that people often write include not enough money, being tied-down by financial and family obligations, not having the right training or know-how, not having enough time, and not having had the right opportunity.

To move forward in creating the life you want you need to eliminate the obstacles on your list. Lets look at each of these most common obstacles and what can be done to deal with them. As we look at them, we'll review them as if this was a business instead of your life.

"Life is what happens to us while we're making plans."
John Lennon

If you don't have enough money, you need to evaluate why. In a business it means that expenses are greater than or equal to the sales and there is no profit available for expansion and sustainability.

At the personal level this happens because either you're living beyond your means (expenses are greater than income,) you don't have a structure for managing your money, you spend on things that aren't necessary, or you have no plan or process for building financial assets. Which of these describes you?

For a business I look at the total net profit and determine how much of it can be allocated to growth and development and how much needs to be invested to keep the business sustainable and viable.

Are you constrained by financial and/or family obligations? If yes, what are your options for changing those constraints? Can you work toward your dreams and change those levels of obligation so that eventually you can achieve the life you want? Remind yourself of why and how you got into your current situation. Was it because you decided to put your dreams on hold, or did you just allow it to happen? Understanding your behavior is key to understanding how and why things happen to you.

If you don't have the right training or know-how to pursue your dream, make a plan to get it. Resources are abundant. Books are free at the library and the Internet is full of free information. If you need formal training look into programs that are available where you live. You will find many affordable options.

Also look into clubs or groups you can join where you'll be with people who have knowledge in the area you want to learn. You'll pick up an amazing amount of wisdom and insider information that will help you. Plus, you'll begin to feel more confident in your ability to pursue your dream.

Eliminating the obstacles may seem daunting when you look at your list. But tackle each one with small steps and little by little the obstacles will disappear. Here's an example of how I took small steps that eventually got me to the larger step of fulfilling one of my dreams:

When I did personal branding for myself, one of my unfulfilled dreams was to live in France. To realize that dream included many complicated scenarios. But one of the easy things I could do to prepare myself for that dream was learn to speak French. I bought the *Rosetta Stone* software, the *Berlitz French Phrase Book* and CD, and enrolled in French classes at a local community college.

I also went to the bookstore where I bought a French/English dictionary and found two other books that were most helpful with slang and colloquial French—*Rendez-vous with France*, a point and pronounce guide by Jill Butler, and Peter Mayle's book, *Provence A-Z*. The rush of enthusiasm and fulfillment I got from taking those actions was the encouragement I needed to pursue my dream.

By the time I went to France in 2008 I had overcome one of my biggest obstacles—the language. My first meal in Paris was at Le Train Bleu, the restaurant in Gare de Lyon, while waiting for my TGV train to Avignon. I ordered my meal and spoke to the waiter without any hesitation. If I mangled the pronunciation of the words, he was kind enough to not notice. I discovered that the French love Americans who at least attempt to speak their language.

Look at your list of what prevents you from having the life you want. Think about what you can do now that will get you closer to that life. Take the first steps. They will build your confidence that it can happen.

If you're wondering whether I live in France now, the answer is "No." I spent time there. I looked at homes and real estate prices. I inquired about all the legalities of owning a home and taking up residence, and eventually altered my dream. It turned out that visiting France was enough. I would not have been happy living there.

Some dreams are like that. When you finally make them come true you discover that the dream was better than the reality. That's why I suggested you put the list you wrote in Chapter 4, of what you want your life to be, in pencil.

Chapter 6

Understand Your Misery Index

"If you obey all the rules, you miss all the fun."
Katherine Hepburn

In the world of marketing, products are often sold by focusing on the misery in people's lives.

Have chronic upset stomach? Take this pill.

Need to lose weight? Buy this piece of equipment.

Paying too much for your phone service? Switch to this provider.

Those of us who create advertising know how effective it is to connect with misery. It's the problem/solution approach. In the world of brands, misery really loves company. The next time you're watching TV notice how many commercials focus on some level of misery in order to make you buy the product.

Success doesn't allow for misery.

Success claims that if you have enough of the right stuff, you'll have no misery. Yet success, as most of us experience it, often brings stress, anxiety, frustration, and demands that cause misery and make us unhappy.

Other people and situations often bring misery to you. Miseries can be huge problems or small annoyances that become huge to you. They make you unhappy or angry. They can quickly overwhelm your life. In your list of what prevents you from having the life you want (Chapter 5) you've already identified some of the miseries in your life.

Many people don't know what they want their lives to be. In fact, many people don't know what they want. This quickly becomes clear in the world of branding. When faced with the challenge of marketing a new brand, companies do research.

Among the processes they use is the focus group. In focus groups consumers tell why they like or dislike something and whether they would buy it. Yet when the company brings the product to market they discover that consumers often don't buy it. That's because people are stuck in the past. They respond to questions by drawing on past experiences. There is no innovation or forward thinking in their responses. This makes their responses unreliable.

The average person resists change. Things that are new and unknown cause people to be confused, apprehensive, and afraid. That same process applies to taking steps to make changes in your life. Doing something different and new can be the best thing that ever happens to you. But to do that you need to face the risks.

> *"Many people don't know what they want until you show it to them."*
> Steve Jobs

Apple, under the direction of Steve Jobs, is considered one of the most innovative companies in the world.

Yet none of their products was something consumers indicated they wanted.

When you look at the lives of people who are responsible for the greatest innovations in the world, you soon discover that there is a common thread. They were misfits, troubled children, dreamers, and non-conformists. Many were ridiculed for their ideas. Steve Jobs is an excellent example.

Thomas Edison is another. Edison's teachers labeled him as "addled" because his mind wandered and he didn't concentrate on his studies. His mother, recognizing his gifts, took him out of public school and home-schooled him.

Edison and Jobs both gave the world products they didn't know they wanted. After having these products, people couldn't imagine ever living without them.

It takes forward thinking to identify and eliminate what makes your life less than you want it to be, and then determine how to achieve the better life you want. It also takes self-confidence to not care what others think of your dreams and ideas.

In addition to what prevents you from having the life you want, also identify . . .

What or Who makes you UNHAPPY?

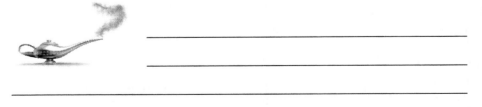

_____

_____

_____

_____

_____

_____

_____

_____

_____

_____

The combination of your answers to this question and your answers to what prevents you from having the life you want, clearly define the problems you need to solve.

Mercedes Lackey, the popular writer of fantasy novels, said the saddest two words in the English language are, "If only." You don't want to live an "if only" life. And you don't have to. All you need is the determination to eliminate the miseries from your life and replace them with what makes you happy.

One of the most common but subtle miseries is boredom. Are you bored with your life? Do you find yourself wondering, "Is this all there is?" Many people are willing to take life as it comes. But eventually all of us get to that point where we wonder if there could or should have been something more. Sometimes the best way to discover what you really want is to try different things.

In the movie *Julie and Julia,* based on the real lives of Julie Powell and Julia Child, both characters were bored with life. Julia Child didn't know what to do when she and her husband moved to Paris. She felt useless.

She tried learning to play bridge and designing hats. Hated both. Finally she tried cooking. She loved it.

Despite no encouragement from the Cordon Bleu cooking school she attended, she persevered and eventually studied cooking with master chef Max Bugnard. Julia Child said that until she discovered cooking she really wasn't interested in anything. Cooking became her passion.

Her passion for cooking led her to join Cercle des Gourmettes, a women's cooking club. There she met Simone Beck and Louisette Bertholle. Together they created a book to teach French cooking to Americans. The cookbook led to a TV show for Child, and that show and cookbook changed American attitudes toward food and cooking.

Julie Powell, who also loved cooking, spent a year making all the recipes in Julia Child's cookbook as an escape that gave her a purpose beyond the daily grind of her emotionally demanding and stressful job. She turned that purpose into a blog, and eventually wrote a book about the experience.

Both Julie Powell and Julia Child created their own successful outcomes, and they did it to overcome a misery in their lives.

> *"The greater part of our happiness or misery depends on our disposition and not our circumstances."*
> *Martha Washington*

Getting rid of the stuff that brings you down and makes you unhappy is something only you can do. The problem/solution approach gives you the process for doing it. Take your list of what makes you unhappy, frustrated, angry, or stressed and answer these four questions about each item:

What causes this to happen to me?

Why do I let this happen?

How can I stop this from happening?

What will happen if I stop it?

Some things will be easy to change now that you've identified them. Others will be much more complex. Perceptions of misery, just like happiness, usually revolve around the five major circumstances of life—money, job/career, time, relationships, and health. But it is often the small things that impact you the most.

A positive attitude is helpful but it won't eliminate the misery from your life. In fact, a positive attitude often prevents you from making the changes you need to make. With a positive attitude people are often lulled into thinking that things will get better. Things will improve. We hope for the best. Because of it people with positive attitudes often stop there, and never take the actions they need.

Thinking positive can be counter-productive because it suppresses the intensity of the need to make changes. Like Scarlet O'Hara in *Gone With the Wind*, we think that tomorrow is another day, and we put off taking actions needed today because we're optimistic that we'll have new opportunities later. Eventually we put off actions for a longer and longer period of time.

This is another example of how using a business strategic planning process can get you out of procrastination and into action. A business can't put off making necessary changes that are critical to the well-being of the company. If they do, they're out of business.

When you think of yourself as a brand, and the success of your brand becomes your top priority, you realize that you need to take action now to get rid of your problems by replacing them with solutions.

Prioritize the things that make you unhappy by those easiest to eliminate to those that are most difficult to eliminate. This is the beginning of your personal strategic plan to achieving your successful outcome. Start with the easiest and develop the solution for getting it out of your life. Put your solution into action. Continue doing this until you've eliminated everything on your list.

As you look at the connections between what makes you happy and what makes you unhappy, it becomes clear that when you eliminate all the things on your misery list you create opportunities for happiness.

Chapter 7

Love What You Do

"Most folks are about as happy as they
make up their minds to be."

Abraham Lincoln

The Bureau of Labor Statistics released numbers on how we spend a typical day. The typical 24-hour period includes:

8.8 hours for work

7.6 hours for sleep

2.5 hours for leisure

1.2 hours caring for others

1.1 hours for household activities

1.1 hours for eating/drinking

1.7 hours for everything else we do

You spend more of your awake time on work than all other functions combined. Therefore, if you are working at something you don't love, you are spending the largest amount of your time being miserable.

Confucius said that a man who loves what he does never works a day in his life. Work is an essential part of life. It provides income and resources for your needs and desires. When you do work that you love you create fulfillment for your life. When you do work you dislike, you enslave yourself to a wage.

Our careers, jobs, and professions are more than just livelihoods. They are part of our personal brands. We are defined by what we do. In social situations the two most frequent questions asked by someone we meet for the first time are, "Where are you from?" and "What do you do?"

When people retire one of the biggest adjustments they make is figuring out who they are now that they are no longer employed.

My father started his own business, a retail shoe store with a shoe repair department, after being discharged from the Army when WWII ended. He loved it. It was his passion. He worked long hours and not once did I ever hear him complain.

When I was five he started to let me help him in the business by doing little things. It made me feel very grown up. I continued to work in Dad's business until I left home for college. I learned about inventory, accounting, cash flow, customer service, purchasing, and advertising. But mostly I learned that it's important to do work that you love.

My dad was disappointed that I didn't stay and make a career with him, to eventually take over the business he started. But he understood I needed to pursue my passion. When he was 62 he sold his business and retired. Within months he had turned his woodworking hobby into a new business. For years my brothers, sisters and I received gifts at Christmas that were Dad's handcrafted items.

Eventually he stopped that and it wasn't long until he took a part time job helping at the local funeral home when there were more funerals than they had staff to manage. He also drove the 60 mile trip to the airport to transport the deceased. He stayed with that job for a number of years.

He is now 91. He's been "retired" for 29 years. I call him nearly every night to see how he's doing. On Monday nights I can't call until 9:30 because he has chorus practice. He has been singing with a men's choral group for 60 years. They perform at churches, schools, nursing homes, retirement communities, private dinners or parties, and public events. Recently he told me he's going to be really busy this year because their schedule is booked with an event every week. He loves to sing.

When I visit my dad, and we go out to eat or shop, we always encounter people who know him. They all stop to talk, inquire how he is, and tell him he's looking really good. Nearly everyone has a "shoe" story about something he did for them when they were customers in his store. Owning the shoe store is a thing of the past, but it is a permanent part of who he is because he touched so many lives.

I believe that my father has lived to be a healthy 91 years young because he has loved what he does his entire life. He is consistently happy, cheerful, and optimistic. He is totally independent and still lives in the house he and my stepmother built after most of us kids were grown and gone. He's been alone for three years, and has learned to cope with that. He has a wide circle of friends who invite him to dinner or go out to eat with him. He stays happy and busy.

Most of us stay busy. But we don't stay happy.

The U.S. is the most overworked nation in the world. And most people are not happy in their work. 70% of two-parent households have both parents working. We are the only civilized country that does not have a parental leave program so parents of newborns can stay home during critical early childhood development years. In European countries new parents get 20 weeks of leave.

Americans work 137 more hours each year than the Japanese, 260 hours more each year than the British, and 499 hours more than the French. When we're working that much, it is essential that we love what we do because it is such a major part of our lives.

> *"The people who get on in this world are the people who get up and look for the circumstances they want, and, if they can't find them, make them."*
>
> George Bernard Shaw

A key part of creating the life you want is living a life that makes you happy. What makes you happy? Are you spending your time doing things that make you happy? If not, how can you change that? Write down . . .

What Makes YOU Happy?

_____

_____

_____

_____

_____

_____

_____

_____

_____

_____

_____

_____

_____

_____

As you look at what makes you happy think about the statistics at the beginning of this chapter. How much of your time is spent doing things that make you happy? How can you change your life so you have more time for what makes you happy? If you aren't happy in the work you do, make a plan to find work that inspires you and nurtures your passions.

There is no age limit for starting to create the life you want. Whatever you want to do, you can. You are never too young or too old to change careers or change lifestyles to accommodate the career you want. You just need to start.

Ian Fleming was 44 when he wrote his first James Bond novel, "*Casino Royale.*"

Fleming had difficulty getting his first book published. With the help of friends he finally got a publishing house to print the first book, but they did it without any confidence or enthusiasm for its potential success. They were so wrong. It took three press runs to fill the demand for copies when the first Bond book came out. Whatever you do, don't let the so-called "experts" kill your dreams.

Fleming died at the age of 56 and his last two Bond books were published posthumously. He never knew that his literary character became a cultural icon that survived many reincarnations and was still popular 60 years after the first book. And millions of enthusiastic James Bond fans are grateful that at age 44 Fleming changed his career.

A few years ago I was white water rafting on the Lehigh River. There were only three people on the raft. Me, my friend, and the guide. During our conversations I discovered that my guide was college trained in computer sciences. He had pursued that career on the advice of his high school guidance counselor because he had the aptitude and was assured it would land him a good-paying job. The counselor was right. After college he got a good job in the computer field. There was only one problem. He hated it.

In school he was always involved in sports. He was athletic and loved the outdoors. Being stuck in a windowless office was torture for him. So at the age of 25 he quit his computer job and took a job as a river guide for a white water rafting company. In the winters, when there were no river tours, he worked at a ski resort.

He told me he was now earning less and had downsized to a smaller apartment, but got up every day looking forward to what he was going to do. He loved it! Even more, by getting a job doing what he loved he was surrounded by others who loved it too. He met a girl who shared his passion for the outdoor life and his dreams, and he was happier than he ever imagined.

For both Fleming and my river guide, pursuing their passion wasn't about money. It was about doing something they loved.

If you're doing something you don't love because you can make more money, look at how to change your lifestyle so you can live as you want and do what you love.

A friend told me about a friend of his who went through a nasty divorce. His ex-wife's lawyers made sure she got everything. He went from living an upscale life with all the trappings to being reduced to near poverty.

In looking for a place to live that he could afford with the meager amount of wages he had left, he rented a small 2-room cabin on a lake. The cabin had basic plumbing, was heated with a wood stove, no AC for summer, but it did have electricity. What made it appealing was that it was on a lake with good fishing, and the man loved to fish.

He settled into his much smaller new life and discovered that he became happier with every day that passed. He didn't miss the big house that he had worked so hard to acquire. He didn't miss all the possessions that filled that house, or the status symbol automobile that went to the ex-wife. He had very little and he loved it.

Many people work at jobs they don't like to buy things they don't really need. When you look at the list of what makes you happy, think about how you could have all of what's on your list by doing something you love.

Chapter 8

Control the Need for More

"Being rich is having money. Being wealthy is having time."
Margaret Bonnano

You know the phrase "Money can't buy happiness." It's true.

But having money is definitely better than not having it.

The real problem is that most of us allow money to trap us in lives that require us to spend our time acquiring more money so we can afford those things we thought would make us happy, only to discover that they don't.

It's a spiral that pulls you in the wrong direction. It happens to everyone.

Look at Elvis. Elvis Presley had it all.

The king of rock 'n roll had looks, talent, fame, fortune, and fans. He was idolized, celebrated, and revered around the world. He personified the American dream. Born into a poor Mississippi family he became so famous and successful you need only to say "Elvis" and everyone around the world knows who you're talking about.

Elvis is regarded as one of the most important figures of 20th century culture. He had everything. Yet his life ended in agony, misery, and unhappiness. He became addicted to drugs. His handsome face and physique, that made girls and women swoon with desire, became bloated and overweight. He became isolated and friendless. On August 16, 1977, he was discovered alone and unconscious on the bathroom floor of his Memphis, Tennessee mansion, and later that day was pronounced dead at Baptist Memorial Hospital.

Elvis was caught in the spiral of the success myth. He had everything and yet he had nothing that brought him true happiness.

In 2006, the year I started developing my personal branding process, Elvis's home was declared a National Historic Landmark. Even in death, Elvis is one of the top earning departed celebrities, with income last year of $52 million. Elvis became a hugely successful brand. But it wasn't a brand that made him happy in his life. Elvis needed to change his brand, but was caught in its trap—a realization he put into a hit song.

Celebrities in the worlds of entertainment, sports, and politics self-destruct all the time. These are people with immense success and wealth. People like Tiger Woods. And people like Elvis. Their money, fame, and success give them a false sense of power and control.

To be in control of your success it is essential to realize that success and happiness are not determined by money. Money is only a tool you use to reach and sustain your ideal life. You may be surprised at the difference between how much you think you need and how much you really need to be happy.

> *"Too many people buy things they don't need to impress people they don't like."*
> *Will Smith*

The part of the success myth that is easiest to buy into is that if we have more, we'll be happier. But it does not take spending to assure a fulfilled life. The expression "less is more" may be true for you as you develop your personal brand.

Many people are confronted by this reality when they become victims of natural disasters, marketplace disasters, or health problems. Hurricanes, floods, and tornados can take away everything in just hours or days. Economic recessions and depressions cost jobs, force businesses to close, erode investments and nesteggs, and reduce the value of your money. A serious illness or disease takes away the ability to work while creating overwhelming costs that wipe out financial stability.

People who are faced with re-building after a disaster, who had to adjust their standard of living due to economic or job loss, or have had their normal world turned upside down by an illness, often realize that so much of what they thought they needed wasn't important after all. When life is reduced to survival, prioritized by food, shelter, and health, the luxuries we indulge in become insignificant.

Hopefully you have never been a victim of any of these acts. But thinking about them should get you thinking about your attitude when it comes to money.

In America, spending money is one of the biggest leisure pastimes. Americans shop for fun. We collect stuff. Almost anything you can think of is collectable. The stuff we buy but don't really need falls into the category of leisure consumable goods.

Buying leisure consumable goods is big business. It keeps our economy strong. But the reality is, just how much stuff do you need? When you can only wear one pair of jeans at a time, and almost every home is equipped with a washing machine, and every small town and city has laundromats, why do you need a dozen pairs of jeans?

Before you can look at the significance of money in your strategic plan, you need to understand the motivation for all this spending—much of it driven by innovation and advertising. This frenzy to buy things we don't need has five dimensions. Which of them describes you?

1. **We buy things to reward ourselves.** Shopping and getting something new can make you feel good if you've had a bad day. Or, perhaps you've just accomplished something great. You've won an award or gotten a raise. So you buy something to celebrate. Or, sometimes you buy things you don't need because you just feel that you deserve something new. After all, advertising convinces us that we're worth it.

2. **We buy stuff as an investment**. We believe the stuff we acquire will someday have an increased value. When enough people collect the same things, the prices go up due to limited supply. People then buy more to increase the value of their collections. We become convinced that someday we will sell our collections for a substantial amount of money. This perception is reinforced by TV shows like *Antiques Road Show.*

3. **The things we buy are an extension of who we are.** Just as people can be defined by success in their jobs, another way of defining your individual brand is by success in what you have.

You can become a celebrity in the niche market of people who collect or have the same things you do. A good friend of mine is a single man with two cars. One is a classic Corvette he mostly drives for show and to enter in car shows. The Corvette is one way he defines himself.

4. **We spend money to secure a place of prestige and social prominence.** From the size and location of our homes, or the number of homes we have, the cars we drive, places we've been, the foods and beverages we consume, the type of clothing we wear, and the activities we engage in, we brand ourselves more to impress the marketplace rather than to fulfill our own personal desires. Keeping up with, or one step ahead of, the Joneses can require constant spending.

5. **We can't resist bargains. Shoppers love to "save" money on their purchases.** Most of us, however, are lured into buying things we don't need through sales, discounts, coupons, bogos (buy one get one free) and other price enticements. We boast about our great bargains, are pleased with ourselves for being savvy shoppers, and tell our friends how much we saved. When we buy things we don't need, and may never or rarely use, just because the price was right, we're wasting our money.

What would you do if a disaster took away your stuff? Anytime you lose something you spent money to acquire, you start to re-think whether it is really worth acquiring it for a second time.

As you look at the lists you've made in this book, what you want your life to be, what prevents you from having that life, what makes you happy, and what makes you unhappy, how does money figure into your lists?

If you really want to achieve the life you want, before making a purchase ask yourself this question: "How does buying this get me closer to the life I want?"

It is not my purpose in this book to tell you how to spend your money. I want you to define what "having it all" really means to you. Put that into perspective with what you are doing with the money you have and the money you think you need.

Success is to stop spending on anything that doesn't directly relate to what creates the life you want and therefore defines happiness for you. When we look at spending as part of strategic plans for businesses, we define successful spending by ROI—return on investment. Most people have more money than they realize, and need less money than they think. It is the choices they make with their money that keep them feeling financially challenged or stressed.

In developing your personal strategic plan, the return on investment for the money you earn and the way you spend it should be measured by how it gets you to the life you want. If you are spending on things that are not achieving that goal it is not a good return on investment for you.

Businesses use a cash flow sheet to show money in, money out, and money that contributes to profit. I encourage you to create a cash flow sheet for your personal life. It's very easy to do with a computer and Excel. You don't need to use accounting software.

A sample personal cash flow sheet is provided for you on pages 68 and 69. Set up your cash flow sheet with 12 monthly columns spread horizontally across the top of the sheet. A vertical column at the left of the sheet is where you list all of your sources for income and expenses.

SAMPLE: Personal Cash Flow

SOURCE	JAN	FEB	MAR	APR	MAY	JUN	JUL	AUG	SEP	OCT	NOV	DEC
INCOME												
Salary#1												
Salary#2												
Interest												
Investments												
Gifts												
Refunds												
TOTAL:	Add all income sources.											
EXPENSES												
Fixed:												
Mortgage												
Heat												
Electric												
Internet												
Phone												
Car Insurance												
Water												
Trash												
Taxes												
TOTAL:	Add all fixed expenses.											
NET INCOME:	Subract fixed expenses from total income.											
Essential:												
Groceries												
Gasoline												
Car Repairs												
HH Insurance												
Clothinng												
Hair Cuts												
Toiletries												
Prescriptions												
Doctors												
TOTAL:	Add all essential expenses.											
ADJUSTEDNET	Subtract the essential total from t he net income.											

SOURCE	JAN	FEB	MAR	APR	MAY	JUN	JUL	AUG	SEP	OCT	NOV	DEC
Discretionary:												
Entertainment												
Eating out												
Books, Mags												
Games, Sports												
Vacations												
Birthday Gifts												
Holiday Gifts												
Donations												
HH Purchases												
Wine, Beer												
Garden/Plants												
Home Improve												
TOTAL:	Add all money spent on discretionary items.											
PROFIT:	Subtract discretionary from adjusted net. This is the money you have to contribute to savings & the life you want.											
	Note: There is no place for credit card payments. If you have those payments, they will be in the Fixed Expenses.											
	There is also no place shown for car payments. If you have one or two of those each month, they will also be in the Fixed Expenses.											

The first section should be your income. Have a separate line for each income source.

Your expenses should be separated into 3 categories. The first category will be all of your essential expenses - those things you are required to pay each month such as rent/mortgage, electric, etc. The next category of expenses should be the essential expenses you can control based on your lifestyle and purchase choices. These include items such as food, gas, and personal products. The final category of expenses is for discretionary purchases. These are the items you spend on that are not part of life's necessities.

The list of expense sources will vary for each person, so use my chart as a guideline to help you get started.

At the end of each month, enter the amount of money you've earned or received from your income sources. Then enter all the money you've spent in your expense sources. I recommend you have a drawer or a box where you put receipts for all those items you purchase with cash. You will have bank records to refer to for items purchased with checks or debit/credit cards.

Put formulas in your spreadsheet that add up all your income, add up your expenses in each of the 3 categories, total all those expenses, then subtract the amount spent from the amount received. That is your cash flow for each month. If you are earning more than you spend, you have money to put toward the actions you'll take to create the life you want. If you spend more than you earn, you have a negative cash flow. You need to adjust your lifestyle and spending to get it under control.

> *"There are plenty of ways to get ahead. The first is so basic I'm almost embarrassed to say it: spend less than you earn."*
>
> *Paul Clitheroe*

When you keep track of everything you spend for one year, by category, you will be amazed at where your money goes. 69% of American households live paycheck to paycheck, yet they engage in a lot of wasteful spending. If you are one of those households, you'll have no money available to change that situation. To evaluate your spending, start by answering this question:

What do YOU have you NEVER, or SELDOM use?

_____

_____

_____

_____

_____

_____

_____

_____

_____

_____

_____

_____

_____

Entire industries have evolved to help us de-clutter all the stuff we don't need or use.

Where I live there are 120 self-storage facilities where people rent space to keep stuff they have no room for in their homes. The off-site storage boom is everywhere. TV shows such as *Auction Hunters* and *Storage Wars* show people bidding on stuff that has been abandoned or left in unpaid storage units.

In the service industry there are many businesses devoted to helping people clean and organize closets, attics, basements, garages, and cupboards to identify what they really need, organize it so they can find it, and get rid of what they don't use.

All of this supports one undeniable conclusion: spending can easily get out of hand. What do your closets, cupboards, cabinets, and clutter say about you? Look at the list you just created and you'll see a picture of all those things you can't say "no" to. Keep that list so you don't keep adding to it.

There are four steps you can take to creating a steady accumulation of wealth. Not billionaire wealth, but the steady, slow accumulation of more money. If you follow these steps you will make your money work for you.

1. Cut up and cancel all credit cards.

Instead of credit get a debit card that takes money directly out of your bank account. If you think you can't live without your credit cards you're most likely living beyond your means. Here's why this is such an important first step.

- Credit cards make it easy to buy things you don't need and can't afford. They motivate impulse buying because you can make a purchase without having to think about it. With a debit card, you still don't need to carry cash but you need to think about how much money you have in the bank before you use it. When you realize your bank account is low, and you know you have bills to pay, you realize that nifty gadget or really neat item isn't a must-have purchase for you.

- 59% of credit card holders carry a balance from month to month. If you are one of them, think about this: You are giving your hard earned money in interest paid each month to a financial company that was most-likely bailed out by your tax dollars in both the Bush and Obama administrations because they didn't handle your money well in the first place. Why would you do this?

- Credit card companies are ruthless in their advertising to entice you to spend by offering rewards and "cash back" incentives. These are phony. They are offered for one reason only: to get you to charge large amounts on your card. The rewards and cash back are miniscule amounts of money in comparison to the amount you give them in interest if you carry a balance. They know that the more you charge, the more likely it is that you'll not be able to pay off your balance each month. That gets them the interest money they count on. Americans pay $49 billion to credit card companies in interest each year.

From my experience Capital One is the worst offender, and they are the worst of the credit card companies to deal with if you get in trouble with a balance you can't pay. There is an entire website devoted to consumers' complaints about their treatment by Capital One, many of which include being sued and taken to court. They are rigid and ruthless. The correct answer to "What's in your wallet?" should be—no credit cards.

In the 40 years I worked in advertising and marketing I did strategic plans and branding for hundreds of products and businesses. But I never accepted a bank or credit card company as a client because of what I feel are the shoddy practices and treatment of consumers that they engage in.

2. Pay yourself each month.

In the essential expense section of your cash flow sheet, put a line for yourself. Every time you get a paycheck, re-pay some of it to you. If you get paid biweekly that's 26 paychecks. If you take just $50 of each paycheck and pay yourself, at the end of the year you'll have $1,300.

Put the money aside. You can open a special bank savings account for it, or, since banks are paying virtually no interest on savings, you can just keep it someplace out of sight at home. Put it in a shoe box, in an envelope in a drawer. Just be sure to put it aside. This is the beginning of your "dream fund," the money you will use to help you realize those dreams you identified earlier. It can also be an emergency fund should something happen that is a true emergency. You will need to have the control to not take from this money for any other reason.

3. Don't buy anything you haven't put on a list.

Keep a tablet in a handy place or use a note app on your smart phone or iPad. Get in the habit of making and using lists. Every time you think of something you need, write it on the list. Don't go to a store without a list. When you do go to a store, buy only what you put on the list.

Make a different list for every category of need by the store you shop at, such as Grocery Store, Home Store, Department Store, Drug Store. Or if it works better for you, keep your lists by store names of the places you shop. If you get your food, household goods, clothing, and drug store items all at one store, such as WalMart, make one list for your WalMart shopping. The key thing is to only buy what's on the list!

Here's why this works. It prevents you from making impulse purchases. Stores are experts at finding ways to convince you to buy things you don't need by making offers you can't refuse. I know. I've created offers for a lot of businesses. I've tested them to see what works best. I've taught workshops to businesses about how to increase sales through the use of offers.

Bogos (buy one get one free) are the most powerful. Who can resist something for free? But if you buy something you don't need, to get more of it for free, you've wasted your money. Two-fers (two for the price of one) is actually the same deal presented differently. Bonus buys, discounts, coupons, and closeouts are all good for you only if you are in need of the items in the first place. People who do extreme couponing boast about the amount of savings. But you aren't saving, regardless of the price, if you spent money for something you don't need.

Another way lists control spending is they make you aware of how you could be making better buying decisions. Americans spend $29 billion each year on candy and $76 billion on soft drinks. Candy and soft drinks have no nutritional value so they are not essential food purchases. I'm not telling you to stop buying them. But making lists of what you need will help you see where you might be able to reduce expenses by eliminating or reducing the money spent on things of little value

> *"The odds of going to the store for a loaf of bread and coming out with only a loaf of bread are three billion to one."*
>
> *Erma Bombeck*

4. Keep a running tab of your unnecessary spending.

Start with the list you made in this chapter of all those things you have but never use. Put a price next to them of what you think you spent for them.

Next, take some time on a rainy weekend to go through your cupboards, cabinets, and closets with notebook and pen in hand. Write down all the things you have that you don't use. You'll find that many of these are things you decided to buy because you were in a store while there was a special sale or discount and you figured you couldn't pass up the great bargain.

Sales make us think we're savvy shoppers. When we see a shirt in a store marked down from $29.99 to $11.99 we snap it up and compliment ourselves on making a great buy. We never stop to think about whether or not we need the shirt. Go through everything. Check your clothes, toiletries and cosmetics, tools and hardware, kitchen items, bookshelves, jewelry boxes, and anything else. Do a complete household inventory.

Businesses do inventory as a regular part of controlling expenses. Now that you're staying on top of your personal spending with a business-type cash flow sheet it is important that you take inventory as well. When you've finished this list of stuff, put the price next to it that you think you paid.

The final part of this is your pantry and refrigerator. Any time you throw away bread, milk, yogurt, fruit, vegetables, or leftovers that have gone bad, write it on a list labeled as Food Waste. If you've thrown out canned or bottled goods because they're past their expiration date put them on your list too. Write what you paid for each item. [Keep your grocery receipts for a month so you can check the exact price.]

Look at how many of the items in your monthly grocery purchases get thrown out. When you put food in the garbage it's the same as putting dollars in your garbage disposal.

Add up the amount of money you've spent for things you don't need. Imagine how much closer you could be to having the life you want if you had that money.

A recent consumer study found that the average American household throws out $40 of food each month. That's $480 per year of unnecessary spending, and that's just for food. *Business Insider's* money report estimates that **Americans waste about a half trillion dollars every year in unnecessary spending.**

When you total all the money you've spent, and are still spending, on unnecessary purchases you'll be astonished. If taking a 2-week vacation each year is part of the life you want, and you aren't doing it because you can't afford it, you probably just realized that you can. All you need to do is change the way you manage your money.

The biggest benefit of controlling your need for more is that you end up having more money! When you become aware of how you manage money you've empowered yourself to do it better. Having money put away is much more fulfilling than having a lot of stuff put away. Money gives you freedom from worry that stuff can't. And it gives you the freedom to create your ideal life.

Chapter 9

Discover Your Purpose

"If you don't stand for something you'll fall for anything."
Michael Evans

When you described what you want your life to be did you include anything that gave purpose to your life? Putting yourself first isn't about being selfish. It's about taking care of yourself so you can fulfill your dreams. Included in those dreams, do you have a goal that will benefit others? Do you have a goal that sets a positive example for others?

Businesses create mission statements. The mission statement is a compass that keeps the business true to the purpose it strives to achieve. Mission statements are part of the business plan. They're shared with employees so they understand the big picture.

For many businesses the mission is to be the best in their field—the best quality, service, and price. For others the mission is to develop and create products that help improve peoples lives. Some have the mission to be the most respected company in their industry. Some have philanthropy and altruism as their mission, dedicated to supporting and promoting causes they believe in.

There are many ways to have purpose in the description of your life.

You may want time to volunteer for causes you believe in, to help those less fortunate than you, to use your expertise and experience to help others, or to nurture and support people you love.

You may want money to contribute to organizations that do good deeds, to exert influence with decision makers about things that are important to you, to help with research and advancement to find solutions to threats and diseases, or to endow and sustain cultural and educational programs.

You may want power and fame that let you personally be in control of leadership decisions that affect change for issues that are important to you. Or you may want to use your power and fame to establish new organizations or foundations devoted to causes and needs you believe in.

Putting yourself first gives you the time, means, and resources to help others.

There are two sides to discovering and creating your purpose. The first is to identify what knowledge, gifts, and talents you have that can be used to fulfill a purpose. The second is to identify what you are passionate about so you can prioritize what purpose will give you the most personal fulfillment and gratification.

For some people fulfillment is measured in the success of helping others, improving the quality of life, and supporting ideas they believe in.

For others personal fulfillment is measured in personal achievement. Just as many companies have "being the best" in their mission statements, for some people their purpose is to be the best. They may want to be the best salesperson in their corporation or the best gymnast in the world. Being the best is a goal that can be reached at many levels.

Sometimes the pursuit of fulfillment and purpose takes a wrong turn. Just as wealth and success can cause people to self-destruct, so can a life dedicated to purpose if your purpose becomes an obsession and you lose your compass.

Lance Armstrong's purpose was to be the best cyclist in the world and to sustain that achievement as long as possible. It drove him. The drive was so strong it helped him survive a life-threatening disease. But the drive to fulfill his purpose eventually destroyed his dream.

Achieving success is only possible when you maintain control. When you lose control you are no longer capable of fulfilling your purpose. Lance Armstrong lost control. He cheated. Instead of a life of purpose he created a life of deceit.

> *"People take different roads seeking fulfillment and happiness. Just because they're not on your road doesn't mean they've gotten lost."*
>
> *H. Jackson Brown, Jr.*

Defining your purpose is another part of defining your brand. It adds depth to who you are. It helps you find more opportunities to be with like-minded people. People who share the same purpose help you multiply the results you can achieve. To help you discover your purpose, answer the following question:

What causes, issues, problems, or beliefs are IMPORTANT TO YOU?

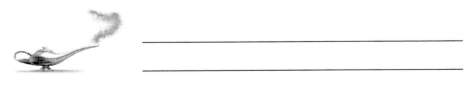

_____

_____

_____

_____

_____

_____

_____

_____

_____

_____

_____

_____

_____

_____

_____

_____

Take your list of causes and issues and prioritize it by numbering 1 as the most important, and the others as 2, 3, 4, etc. in descending levels of importance to you.

In creating your ideal life, what will most enable you to fulfill your purpose? Time, money, prestige, influence?

Now consider how you can fulfill your purpose by answering this question:

What knowledge, expertise, or talent do YOU HAVE that you can use to achieve the purpose in your life?

_____

_____

_____

_____

_____

_____

_____

_____

_____

_____

_____

_____

_____

Sometimes we have expertise and talents we don't recognize. That's because we use them every day and they become ordinary to us. It's just who we are. We fail to see that they make us special and unique.

My grandmother had a talent for quilting. She had an entire room in her house filled with boxes of fabric remnants she got for free from the local shirt factory in our town. The factory made men's shirts and women's blouses so there were fabric pieces and remnants of all patterns, fabrics, and colors. These boxes of fabric pieces were a storehouse of treasure for her.

Every time I went to my grandma's house one of the first things she did was show me the progress she made on the quilt she was currently making. Every piece in the pattern was sewn by hand. Often I would sit beside her while she hand-stitched the individual design elements for a quilt and would use her pattern to cut pieces in the appropriate shape from the remnants for her to stitch.

Grandma was a member of the quilting circle at her church. One day a week women would gather and work together to make quilts. The patterned quilt tops were hand-sewn by each woman at their homes, then brought to the church to have the batting and bottom pinned to the top so the actual hand-quilting stitches could be done. Each woman took a seat around the large quilting frame and sewed her stitches for her section of the quilt. These handcrafted quilts were works of art.

Quilting was just one of my grandmother's passions, but it was the one I think she enjoyed the most.

My stepmother also had a talent for quilting. By the time we kids were all grown and out of the house, and she finally had time to indulge her talent, the shirt factory had closed. Clothing was now being manufactured in China, India, and Bangladesh. So she didn't have the free resource that was available to my grandmother, but she found ways to keep supplied with fabric pieces and remnants for her quilts.

Like my grandmother, she also joined the women's quilting circle at the church and every Wednesday gathered with her friends to spend the day making beautiful quilts. My dad bought her a quilting frame that she set up in the basement family room of the house. That's where she spent most of her time. She loved quilting. It was her passion. And like my grandmother, when I would go home to visit, my stepmother would love to show the new quilt she was working on and the ones she had finished since my last visit.

In my lifetime these two women, along with their friends, made thousands of handmade quilts. The beauty, quality, and workmanship of each quilt was outstanding. They could easily have been sold for hundreds or thousands of dollars each. Instead they were given away to people in need through local charities and church mission work around the world. There were countless hours of manual labors of love done not for monetary profit, but for the fulfillment and satisfaction of helping others. Making quilts was a way they used their talents for a purpose in their lives.

> *"If we all did the things we are capable of, we would astound ourselves."*
> Thomas Edison

Neither my grandmother nor stepmother is still living. I've lost them both. But I have three beautiful quilts lovingly handmade by my grandmother. I have four beautiful quilts lovingly made by my stepmother. They are treasures to me, worth far more than any money someone would pay for them.

There is one quilt I cherish a bit more than the rest. It was one of the last my stepmother made. It's the Grandma's Flower Garden pattern. The colors are vibrant. There are no two flowers the same. My dad cut out all the pattern pieces, and my stepmother hand-stitched the pieces and did the quilting. It is the only quilt they made together.

There are so many talents we each have that are unique just to us. What talents do you have that may seem ordinary to you but actually make you the special person you are?

How will you use them to enhance purpose in your life?

Chapter 10

Find the Perfect Relationship

*"I've never been married. But I tell people I'm divorced so
they won't think there's something wrong with me."*

Elayne Boosler

More than $1.4 billion is spent each year on the purchase of romance
novels. 62% of women buy romance novels which may not surprise
you. But you might be surprised to learn that 44% of men also buy
romance novels.

239 romance authors have made the best-seller list.

The online world is full of sources for romance. Matchmaker websites
promise the ideal way to find your perfect mate. Sites are focused on
people by age, religion, nationality, geography, favorite pastimes, wealth,
and even marital status. (There are even sites for married people who
want to have affairs!) There are sites where kids can find potential mates
for their single parents and parents can find potential mates for their
single kids. The digital world is a supermarket of potential romance!

Romance is big business because we all want that perfect relationship.

Finding the right romantic relationship is often a lifetime pursuit. For some the pursuit is never-ending. Some us move from one wrong relationship to another, some of us never find the relationship we want, some of us stay in relationships that are uncomfortable, and some of us give up without ever getting into any relationship. The lucky ones find their soul mates and create wonderful lives together.

You can't have the perfect relationship without first knowing what you want out of life and what makes you happy. When you've identified what that is, you will be ready to add the relationship dimension to your plan.

Being successful in romantic relationships is one of the most challenging pursuits in creating your happiness. Even people who achieve exceptional success in other parts of life often have difficulty at sustaining success in relationships.

Elizabeth Taylor achieved immense success as an actress, an advocate for causes, and a businesswoman. Universal Studios gave her a seven-year acting contract when she was only 8 years old. Her performance in the film *National Velvet*, at the age of 12, catapulted her career and fame. She won two Best Actress Academy Awards.

She also launched successful perfume brands and put her considerable influence behind changing the perception of HIV/Aids, standing by her long-time friend, actor Rock Hudson, who died of the disease. She won the prestigious Jean Herscholt Humanitarian Award for her work.

But Taylor is just as well known for her eight marriages and divorces. Taylor said that what she found to be sexy in a man was what he says and thinks, his personal warmth. She herself was regarded highly for her lack of ego and simple kindness to everyone. But the successful relationship eluded her throughout her life, despite many romantic relationships in addition to her marriages.

Being in the international spotlight made it difficult for Taylor to pursue the quiet "normal" life she wanted. For most of us, however, there is no international spotlight on our lives to interfere with our romance, and yet we still have difficulty finding and creating the perfect relationship.

There are countless books that tell you how to find the perfect person for you. They cover all categories of romance—teenage love, first love, second time around romance, and soul mates. There are books about the dos and don'ts of dating. Some books offer tricks about ways to attract people. Others give advice on recovering from broken hearts, divorce, and breakups so you can try again. There are books that decode love, and explain how the two genders look at love differently.

With all these books already available to you, I feel it is a bit presumptious of me to write a chapter on the subject of the perfect relationship. After all, I'm not a romance expert. I have no degrees in human behavior. And I have no professional experience in advising the lovelorn.

> *"A perfect relationship isn't ever actually perfect. It's just one where no one ever gives up."*
>
> *Anonymous*

What I do have, however, are my own experiences, observations, conclusions, and results.

In my high school and college years I dated more boys than I can remember. I first married at the age of 22 and divorced at the age of 26. Then I dated again. I married the second time at the age of 28. At the age of 55 we separated and at the age of 58 my second divorce was final. That's not a very good track record.

Why was I such a failure at sustaining a relationship? And why are so many others just as challenged as me?

I concluded that with romance, we are so compelled by emotions in the early phases of the relationship process that we disconnect logic and reason from the situation. The euphoria of discovering a new person, and being discovered in return, is what gives credibility to the phrase "love is blind." It's only after we get into a permanent relationship that we regain 20/20 vision.

But we learn from experience.

Although my experience in romance wasn't successful, my experience in business was.

As I worked on the personal branding approach to change my life, I applied it to romance. How did romance and a serious relationship fit into my strategic plan? Why had I made such disastrous decisions about relationships? So I took my lessons from the world of business and applied them to the world of romance.

It worked for me. I think it can work for you.

Instead of giving you advice I'm just going to tell you what I did and how it worked. You can decide if you like my approach and whether you want to try it yourself.

As a business owner, when I needed to hire someone for a new position I created a job description. The job description determined what skill sets and experience were required for the position. As I received job applications I immediately eliminated those that didn't meet the requirements for the job.

When job applicants came in to be interviewed they also were given two personality tests. One was a short test developed by Dale Carnegie that helped me evaluate what type of employee the person would be. The other was a test developed by Dr. Tony Alessandra that told me what kind of person he or she was—what motivated them, how they would interact with others, and what kind of behavior I could expect from them.

You can't ask everyone you date to take a series of tests to apply for the position of your perfect relationship. Or can you?

> *"Being in a relationship is a full time job. So don't apply if you're not ready."*
> *Anonymous*

Why couldn't I adapt the process to help me evaluate what I was really looking for in my romantic relationship, and cut through all the dating behavior to know whether a person I was dating was a good match?

So I started a relationship process using my business approach. The first thing I needed to decide was whether the timing was right to "hire" someone. And if yes, was this a temporary or permanent position. Was I going on dates just to have a good time or was I looking for someone who was relationship material?

After my second marriage of 27 years, most of which was not very happy, I loved my freedom and the single life. I had lots of friends. I was never lonely. But I wanted to try again to find my Mr. Right. The big question was, if I found my Mr. Right, did I want to get married again? I wasn't sure.

So I created my "relationship test" to help me make decisions, just as the Carnegie and Alessandra tests helped me make hiring decisions. I made a list of 10 questions. I used all the dating and marriage experiences of my past to think about what personal attributes and behaviors were important to making a relationship work for me and with me.

I sequenced my list so I would be able to answer the first question after just one date. If I didn't give a positive answer to that question there was no second date.

Each question got me deeper into the dimensions of a relationship and the characteristics that needed to exist for me to make it work. I wasn't judging the people I dated, I was deciding if they were right for me.

My first question was: "How does this person make me feel when we are together?"

It's a good question. It may not be the right first question for you, but here is why it was right for me. I believe that to have a great relationship you need to be with a person who makes you feel good about yourself. I'm not referring to flattery and compliments. I'm talking about deeper feelings. I wanted someone who listened when I talked and made me feel interesting and fun to be with. Physical chemistry doesn't last if you don't genuinely find each other to be interesting people.

I had first dates where my dates spent the entire time talking about themselves and showed little or no interest in what I thought, felt, or did. I actually wondered why those guys asked me out in the first place. I figured it was because they wanted an audience, not a date. The decision for no second date was a no-brainer.

I also wanted a person who was fun. A sense of humor is important to me so I wanted someone who made me feel happy, which is what laughter does. If I went on a first date and there was nothing said or shared that we could laugh about together, there was no second date.

What is the most important characteristic to you? If you write your own relationship questions that will be the first one.

My second question was: "Is this a face I want to see every day?"

This is a round-about way of dealing with the issue of "looks." I phrased my question this way because I know that physical appearance can change as we age. But the way a person looks is a factor in whether there's a strong enough attraction to sustain a committed relationship. I needed to like the way my man looked, but I didn't want to pre-judge by stating he needed to be of a certain height or build, or have a certain color of hair or eyes.

My third question was: "Is this a person I feel I can talk to about anything?"

Over the years I learned that if you are in a relationship where communication is easy and comfortable, regardless of what you are discussing, you can survive anything together. If you can share opinions, whether you agree or disagree, without criticizing or ridiculing the other person, and without getting angry when you disagree, you show respect for each other's judgment. To me that's vital to a healthy relationship.

I've seen many couples where one of the people would totally minimalize the other. My second husband was a master at it. When that exists there is no possibility of real happiness.

The answer to this question also helped me eliminate people with prejudiced attitudes. I believe that I don't pre-judge others in any way. I truly love people. I love meeting new people. When growing up my dad taught me that strangers were just friends I hadn't yet met. He's been right. There was no room in my life for a person with biases, for any reason.

> *"A successful marriage requires falling in love many times, always with the same person."*
> *Mignon McLaughlin*

My fourth question was: "Is this someone I can trust?"

This question was my turning point. Without trust there is no basis for a successful relationship. If the relationship progressed to question number four, and the answer to question four was yes, then I was willing to pursue a committed relationship.

There were six more questions I needed to answer before making a final and total commitment. Each question got me closer to everything that was important to me. I knew that whoever I was dating was also evaluating me. Perhaps not with a list of questions, the way I was, but by whatever yardstick he measured the attributes he was looking for.

I knew there would be a time when we would both know if we had found the right person. Then we could decide what "forever after" would mean for us.

Reading my questions should get you thinking about what your questions should be.

What is important to you in a relationship? It could be many things. Shared interests. The same values. The same religious beliefs. If you are young it could be the same attitudes about having and raising children. What behavior, manners, and habits are important to you? Are health and fitness a priority? What about temperament? Are you looking for someone with ambition, ideas, and education? Is their career choice significant to you?

There are so many things to consider before getting into a relationship. That's why I feel it helps to put them in writing. Make your list of:

What are YOUR Relationship Questions?

_____

_____

_____

_____

_____

_____

_____

_____

_____

_____

_____

_____

When I wrote my questions I was 56 years old. Your questions will reflect what's important to you at your age and stage of life. By phrasing your list as questions it makes you think below the surface. For example, if it's important to you to find someone who is ambitious and will earn a good income, you need to also think more deeply about what that means.

It may mean that you'll end up in a relationship with someone who is a workaholic—married to a career instead of to you. It won't take long for resentments to build if you think he or she doesn't have time for you and you end up being lonely.

Scientific American Mind magazine published a study that concluded the characteristics we say we want in a relationship are often the very things that destroy the relationship. One example was a woman who wanted a mate with a sense of humor. She found one and married him. Not long into the marriage she became frustrated with him because she felt he was never serious about anything.

As you review your questions think below the surface to what they mean. If you love outdoor sports and activities and want someone who shares that love, what happens to your relationship if a serious injury makes it impossible for that shared enjoyment to continue, whether the injury happens to you or your mate?

As you think more about your questions, here is my fifth one: "Would I be willing to travel around the world with this person?"

Before I could answer "yes" to this question I had to come to terms with many things. In traveling around the world with the person we would be together in close proximity day after day. Could our relationship survive that? Also, when traveling in foreign places you need to deal with new, unknown, and unfamiliar situations. How a person would deal with the unknown was important to me. I had to feel that the person I was considering making a commitment to would be able to think and react in a positive and constructive way if we had to deal with unexpected or serious challenges. And I had to believe we were compatible in this.

My question wasn't about travel. The travel scenario gave me a way to think about behavior in a different context, but the answers in this context told me whether we could survive day to day living together.

> *"My grandmother's 90. She's dating. He's about 93. It's going great. They never argue. The can't hear each other."*
> *Catherine Ladman*

Questions 6 and 7 were: "Would I be comfortable having this person around when I was with my family (especially my son)?" And, "Is this someone I would be proud to introduce to my friends?"

These questions were important because to have a serious relationship the person was going to have to fit into my life. I knew I would have to fit into his as well. If he didn't like my family and my friends the odds are we weren't going to have a successful relationship. If I answered "yes" to both of these questions I was ready for the big one.

Question 8 was the question that would tell me if I was ready for a commitment. It was:

"How would I feel if I knew I would never see or talk to this person again?"

That was my deal-breaker question. If I couldn't imagine a life that didn't include him, it meant I wanted him in my life. By phrasing the question this way it made me think differently than if I had just considered whether I wanted to keep seeing him. My last two questions just reinforced the answer to this one.

This process worked for me. Just before my 58th birthday I finally met someone who made it past question 1. It was four weeks before we had a second date, and another three weeks after that before the third date. Eventually the time lapses between seeing each other grew shorter.

We became engaged when I was 59 and are now planning our future. I'm 62 and he's 63. We've taken our time with this relationship. I've approached it differently than ever before. This time I know I got it right. I think my process will work so you can get it right too.

Chapter 11

Determine the Role of Family and Friends

"If you want to see what your friends and family think of you, die broke, and see who comes to the funeral."

Gregory Nunn

There are an additional two important relationship levels in your life. Family and friends. Without them your life would be lonely. Your success would be empty. The writer Harper Lee said, "You can choose your friends but you can't choose your family." That is the starting point for how to determine what role each plays in the life you want.

Start with family, because they are in your life not by choice, but by circumstance.

Those who are my age remember the ideal family as depicted in old TV shows like *Leave it to Beaver* and *Father Knows Best*. The family TV shows of today demonstrate how much the family structure has changed since then. There is no longer a typical family unit or structure. Perhaps this is epitomized by the popular show *Modern Family*.

Since 2009 *Modern Family* has allowed us to laugh at the unusual, dysfunctional, and untraditional structures that define contemporary families. The show's creators, Christopher Lloyd and Stephen Levitan, call it a mockumentary about family life. The show revolves around three different families, now tied together due to divorces and remarriages.

It's good for us to find an outlet to laugh at these complicated family trees. In reality the blended and multi-tier family units aren't always quite so funny. Around 50% of first marriages end in divorce. 67% of second marriages end in divorce and 74% of third marriages end in divorce. The more we marry the more we divorce.

Divorces impact children. Remarriages often bring two sets of children together as "siblings" who share no common earlier experiences. Later-in-life marriages often involve an older spouse with a previous family starting a new family with a younger spouse, where there are broad differences in the ages of the two sets of children.

Right now 40% of married couples with children are stepcouples where at least one of the parents has a child from a prior marriage. And about a third of all new marriages taking place form a new stepfamily. To say family is complicated is a gross understatement.

Even families that stay in the original dad, mom, and kids structure, with no divorce, don't necessarily produce a loving, supportive unit. Many times the career success of one or both parents leaves little time for success at parenting.

The Baby Boomer generation of parents created the concept of "quality time" to soothe guilty consciences about not having enough time to be with their kids. An extension of the quality time concept was to find other ways for kids to channel their needs and energies. Now we have a whole generation of kids who were raised with virtually every minute of their day scheduled into lessons, sports, activities, and clubs to keep them occupied. Work-weary parents thought they were off the hook because they made sure their kids were just as worn out as they were. Those kids have grown up with a fast-paced hectic lifestyle as their example.

Many have also grown up with stepparents, stepbrothers and stepsisters, and half-brothers and sisters. Many have been shuttled back and forth between two households and had to cope with holidays where enjoyment and celebration were second to decisions about who they would be with and where.

> *"If the family were a fruit, it would be an orange, a circle of sections, held together but separable—each segment distinct."*
>
> *Letty Cottin Pogrebin*

The impact of these family unit changes increases with each demographic group from Baby Boomers to Gen X, to Gen Y and finally to the Millennials. In studies of attitudes and priorities of the Millennial generation, those in their 20s and early 30s, the after effects of these changes are clear.

This demographic group is much more thoughtful and deliberate in their attitudes about marriage and children. As such, the average age for getting married is moving from the early 20s to the late 20s. Many aren't starting families until well into their 30s. When they do have families they're willing to live within a lower level of means in order to have time to be with their children.

Another difference in the attitudes of the Millennial generation is the acceptance for all types of relationships and families. This generation is much more accepting of relationships considered taboo by their grandparents. Most of them are fine with marriages between people of different ethnicities and religions and of same genders. Because of the huge numbers in this generation—more than 70 million—they will have a huge impact on family structure and marriage statistics in the future.

As you look at creating your ideal life, it is important to think about how your family impacts it. How do they fit in? How does what happens to your parents, grandparents, siblings, and children impact what you want your ideal life to be? Are you expected to put those family members before yourself?

Do they support your dreams and encourage you? Or do they criticize and trivialize what you do? Do you feel used and taken advantage of by them or do you feel appreciated and valued by them? Do you spend time with them out of obligation or because you genuinely enjoy being with them?

These are questions you need to answer to determine the role you want your family—parents, children, siblings, and grandparents—to play in your life.

Who are the Family Members in Your Life Who are Important to You?

_____

_____

_____

_____

_____

_____

_____

_____

_____

_____

_____

As you determine the importance of your family in your life, you'll see how they impact your time, money, and career choices. You'll also see how your family relationships can define your personal brand. When you look at the brand attributes you created in Chapter 3, how much importance did you give to the various roles you play in your family structures? (i.e. child, parent, sibling, aunt, uncle, grandparent, grandchild.) How much influence did your family structure have over the brand that defines you?

The family structure in my life was anything but normal, considering that I grew up in the 1950s—the age of the *Leave it to Beaver* family identity. I have an older brother who was 5 when I was born. My mother had a mental breakdown when I was an infant that resulted in permanent mental illness that grew progressively worse unless kept in check by medications. My father was an entrepreneur trying to make a success of his small business and most of his days started at 7 a.m. and ended at 9 p.m. He wasn't the typical 8-5 working dad.

My younger brother came along when I was 8. When I was 9 my mother took him and left. My parents divorced. In my small town in a rural part of Pennsylvania no one else was divorced. I was the only student in my entire school whose parents were divorced. My older brother and I got to choose which parent we would stay with. We both chose our dad. Life with him was what we knew. Life with my mother would have meant a new place to live in a new town. It was too scary.

Normal for me was lots of time with my grandparents, time with my older brother, and time with my dad at his business. When his business expanded he built an apartment on the top floor of the building and that's where the three of us lived while our childhood home was rented to tenants. My older brother and I did visitations with our mom and younger brother.

Eventually, as I entered my teenage years and my older brother was about to graduate from high school, massive changes took place. My dad remarried. We moved back to my family home and my new stepmom, along with four new stepsiblings, moved in. It was no longer the family home I had grown up in. My bedroom now belonged to my younger stepbrother. I shared a bedroom with my two stepsisters.

> *"You hear a lot of dialogue on the death of the American family. Families aren't dying. They're merging into big conglomerates."*
>
> *Erma Bombeck*

During this time my mother moved from Pennsylvania to Florida, taking my younger brother with her. For many years I didn't see either of them. My new half-brother was born when I was 15. I was the middle child of this big blended family. My older brother left for college and I felt like an outsider in a house filled with my stepmother and stepsiblings. My dad was always at his business.

Shortly after my half-brother was born we discovered that my mother's mental illness had become serious. She was hospitalized and my younger brother was in a foster home in Florida. My dad, stepmother, infant half-brother and I got in the car and drove to Florida to get him and bring him home. I don't know which of us, my younger brother or me, was the happiest that we were together again.

Because of all that happened to my two brothers and me, we have what I consider to be an unusually deep level of love and support for each other. We have always tried to be there for one another. When we get together it is impossible for another person to get a word into our conversations. We each live very independent, busy, and different lives. We each inherited our father's drive, ambition, and work ethic, and we could each be described as driven in our careers. We often go for long periods of time without seeing each other. But when we get together, it's as if not a minute has passed.

The stepfamily unit was difficult for us, our stepsiblings, and our parents. We were not The Brady Bunch. One weekend our parents, in an effort to find some way to bring us together, took us to the movies to see *Yours, Mine, and Ours*, a humorous look at two families trying to blend into one. But our parents weren't Lucille Ball and Henry Fonda, and this was our real life, not a movie. It took a tragedy to turn it around.

In June of 1976, my husband (my first husband) unexpectedly appeared in my office. One look at his face told me something was wrong. "Get your things," he said, "We need to go." I asked what was wrong and he didn't want to tell me until we were out of the building, but I insisted I wouldn't leave until I knew why. "Your brother is dead," he said. I asked which brother and learned that the youngest of our blended family, my half-brother, had been brutally killed.

He was nine years old. It was summer. School was out. It was 30 minutes before lunchtime when my dad would come home from his store to have lunch. My half-brother wanted to ride his bike. My stepmother said "No." Lunch was soon ready and he was to wait til after lunch. In that persistant manner that is a specialty of young children, he begged and pleaded until she finally relented, but told him not to ride very far.

He was directly across the street from our house, just a few yards from our front yard, when a large truck came down the street. The driver never saw the child on the bike, so he hit him at full speed. The bike and the boy were hurled through the air and landed three houses up the street. My brother was mercifully dead on impact. My stepmother heard the terrible sounds and came running out of the house. I can't imagine the horror she went through.

A neighbor called my dad who came immediately. My stepmother was paralyzed with grief, unable to cope. A neighbor held her in a tight embrace to keep her from collapsing. My father walked up the street, lovingly and carefully picked up the broken body of his youngest child, and carried it to the funeral home that was only a few more houses further up the street.

Within hours all of us children were back home. We were no longer stepbrothers and stepsisters. We were family. Our parents were heavily medicated, catatonic in their inability to accept what happened.

A constant stream of neighbors came by to share their love and sympathy, and try in some small way to relieve the burden of heartbreak. They brought casseroles, platters, and containers of food. My older stepsister, my older stepbrother's wife, and I took charge. We talked with the neighbors. Explained that our parents weren't able to talk to them, and expressed our deep appreciation for their visit and the food.

Our next door neighbors were Clair and Thelma Lauver. Their youngest child, Nelson, was almost the same age as my half-brother. Nelson Lauver grew up to become a professional speaker. He's known as The American Story Teller. One of the stories he tells is about my father, Wayne Goodling, and that tragic day when his youngest son was killed.

As a result of that fateful day our blended family became just family. The significance of family took on a very new meaning for all of us.

Years later, on a visit from my dad and stepmother when they were in their 80s, I asked them if they knew about Nelson's career, and asked if they wanted to hear his story about them. They said yes.

We sat around my computer and I went to Nelson's website and called up the story. They listened. Both had tears running down their cheeks by the end. It had been 30 years since the only child they had borne together had been taken from them.

[*If you want to hear Nelson's story go to* theamericanstoryteller.com, *click on the stories link, then narrow your search by clicking on the Small Town America category, and click on Goodling, A Story About Neighbors.*]

Friends are the next level of relationships. During our lives we make many types of friends. There are friendships we form through shared interests and associations such as the churches we attend, the organizations we join, and the schools our children attend.

We form friendships with our neighbors where the common basis for the relationship is simply where we live. There are further degrees of the neighborhood relationship. If you have children you'll have stronger friendships with your neighbors who have children. The same can be true of pets. Or, if you have neighbors with children and pets but you don't, you may not form a friendship at all—especially if the neighbor's pet wanders into your yard and leaves evidence that he was there.

We form professional friendships with coworkers, clients, and business associates based on sharing the same work interests. Many of us spend more time with work friends than with long-term friends. Sometimes the work friend relationships can develop into work spouse relationships where two co-workers do so much together, they get familiar with each other's habits, thoughts, and style and function as an at-work couple.

All of these friendships add dimension to our lives and help us define attributes of our personal brands. The perceptions of others, what others say or think about us, the impressions we make, the way we treat others, and the way we show respect and appreciation for others, are all defining brand traits.

But the most significant friendships are the ones that have depth. These are friends you can count on. These are the friends you can call, any day any time, just to talk, or because you want to know how they are, or because you need a friend and you know they'll be there for you.

> *"Friendship is born at the time one of you says, 'What? You too? I thought I was the only one."*
>
> C. S. Lewis

This is your close circle of friends, and most likely it is your smallest circle. Studies show that men spend an average of 10 hours a week with friends while women spend an average of only 7.5 hours a week. Medical studies show that people with close friendships stay healthier. There is healing power in friendship. People with health issues, who also had good friends, are 60% more likely to recover.

Studies about friendship show that over a lifetime a person will form about 396 friendships, of which only 33 will actually be strong ones. They also show that friendship is the glue that holds marriages together.

In today's world it is much easier to stay in touch with friends. Email and social media let us share information and get in touch at will. One interesting way to think about how many friends share your world is to envision a series of concentric circles. In the center circle are your best friends. The next circle is your close friends, then your good friends, then casual friends, and finally your out-of-touch friends. Five circles of friendships.

If something happened in your life, envision it as a drop in the center circle. How long would it take for the ripples of that drop to extend to your outermost circle?

I am fortunate that I have had the same best friend for more than 50 years. I can't imagine my life without her. We talk at least once a week, often more. It hasn't always been this way. Throughout the 50+ years our various marriages and careers have sometimes kept us apart. But we always reconnected as if those years hadn't happened.

We are Yin and Yang—complementary forces that interconnect to form a strong whole. Shortly before my 58th birthday and right after her 58th birthday I almost lost her.

It was the day after Christmas. I was going to her house to exchange our gifts for each other, go out for dinner, and spend the night sitting up gabbing about all the things women talk about when men aren't around. She lives about 15 miles from my dad's house so I stopped to have lunch with him and my stepmom first. When I got ready to leave I called to let her know I was on my way. She didn't answer her phone. I thought it was strange, since she knew I was coming, that she wasn't home. But I got in my car and headed to her place.

> *"A best friend is someone who knows everything about you, still loves you, and doesn't try to change you."*

When I arrived I found a note on her back door, from her sister that said simply, "Carol, something's happened. Call me," signed Suze. And there was a phone number. I called and learned that my best friend had a heart attack and was rushed to the hospital. Fortunately it happened in a public place and she received immediate attention.

She decided to go the funeral of a person in her community that morning. At the end of the funeral she suddenly started to not feel well. She got up to leave but before reaching her car she collapsed. People called the EMS and she was rushed to the local hospital. After a short time there they flew her to a bigger hospital better equipped to take care of her.

As I sat in my car, getting the details from her sister, I was in a panic about how she was. I drove to the hospital. She was in intensive care. I told the staff I was her other sister so I could get into the room. My best friend was heavily sedated but her real sister was there and we stayed until 9:00 that night when the hospital staff made us leave.

The next morning I drove back and was in her room by 10 a.m. She was groggy but awake and we could talk. That's when I learned that she had been undecided about whether to go to the funeral or not. Since I was coming to visit she thought perhaps she should just stay home. To this day we are thankful for her decision to go to the funeral. Had she stayed home she would have collapsed at home with no one to know or call 911. Instead of my arriving at her empty house, I would have arrived and found my best friend dead on the floor.

Life can hang on a single action or decision. When it comes to your friends, answer this question:

Who are the FRIENDS you can't imagine life without?

_____

_____

_____

_____

_____

_____

_____

_____

_____

_____

_____

_____

_____

_____

As you look at this list, consider how these people fit into your dreams and what you want your life to be. Is there a place for them? Do you have a place in their lives? Are you there for each other? Do you help each other achieve your dreams?

My best friend has had a difficult struggle. Her doctor gave her time to recover from the heart attack before scheduling heart surgery. During that time we agreed that as soon as she was recovered from the surgery we would go on a cruise and celebrate.

In the spring of 2011 we took the cruise. We were in a jewelry store in St. Thomas where my friend was shopping for a pair of black diamond earrings. The salesman waiting on us had shown us several different pairs.

We discussed the merits of all and it was obvious to the salesman that she wasn't going to make a purchase unless I approved. He asked if we were sisters and we said no. He said he didn't think so because we don't really have similarities in our looks. But he said there must be something special because of how we interacted and related with each other so easily. We told him we'd been best friends for almost 50 years.

He excused himself and in a couple minutes came back with a bottle of spiced rum and three glasses, and we toasted our friendship. It was a wonderful moment. And yes, he made the sale. He then gave each of us a necklace, the same necklace for both of us. Sterling silver with an aquamarine stone—a gift, he said, for friendship.

Four months later I was traveling in Colorado when I got a phone call from one of our mutual friends and learned that my best friend had cancer. She found out a month after getting back from our cruise. She didn't tell me because she knew I had a trip planned to go out west and she was afraid I would cancel it if I knew. That's what best friends do. Best friends put you and your needs ahead of their own.

She's still battling the cancer. She's been through hell, as any cancer patient knows. She's a fighter and a survivor. Last year we took a trip to the beach for some R&R before she began a new round of chemo and radiation. We talk about the next cruise to celebrate her being cancer free. Every time we think we can make plans for that cruise a new test finds a new tumor. It is a struggle to stay optimistic. She was recently told there is nothing more they can do, and she may have less than a year left.

It makes you realize that life isn't fair. What you cherish most can be taken from you and there is nothing you can do about it. All the money, success, influence, and power you may have acquired means nothing when it comes to friends. You can't buy true friendship.

When you create the plan for your ideal life, when you define what success is for you, remember that you are defined by the kind of friend you are to others. The only way to obtain true friendship is to give it.

Chapter 12

Take Care of Yourself

"You're never too old to become younger."

Mae West

Top brands and successful businesses are the result of careful nurturing. Marketing of the brands and business is a never-ending process. The difference between advertising and marketing is that the first is just about communicating a message in the marketplace. The second is everything you do in the marketplace—the impressions you make, the value you provide to customers, and your reputatation.

You can't let either the brand or the business get tired or worn out. In marketing, one of the quickest ways to destroy a leading brand is to get complacent about it. When that happens a top ranked brand can slowly deteriorate because of a "good enough" attitude.

Are you stuck in a "good enough" level in your life when it comes to taking care of yourself?

You don't have to strive for perfection. It's unattainable and just adds stress. But you can't create the life you want if you don't take care of yourself.

There are four key areas in which you should be taking care of yourself: health, fitness, image, and stress.

The greatest obstacle to being able to live your dreams isn't lack of money, skill, or opportunity. It's not being in good health. Whatever your age, putting yourself first starts with taking care of yourself.

Healthcare in America is a gigantic money machine. Most of the major health insurance providers have had record profits for the past three years, some as much as a 56% increase per year. Their financial reserves are stashed with cash.

Pharmaceutical company profits also continue to rise, as drug companies spend billions on disease-mongering advertising to convince consumers that every ache, pain, and discomfort, regardless of how insignifcant, could be a sign of something worse. They give scary sounding names to common ailments so we'll buy their drugs, and we fall for it. What was advertised as occasional heartburn 50 years ago is now gastro-esophogeal reflux disease.

The best way for each of us to fight this system is to make good health choices through smart eating. Bookstores are packed with titles that niche the world of diets and healthy eating into macro targeted markets. What most of us really need is to forget all the diet gimmicks and just make healthy choices in the types of food we eat and how much we eat.

Fitness is more than health. It's what we do to keep our bodies in good condition.

Think of your personal brand as a car. The food you eat is the fuel for your car. You want a good clean-burning fuel that keeps your car running at peak performance. Fitness is all those things you do to take care of the car to protect the finish, be sure the tires are good, and keep all the parts tuned up and working.

Most of us take better care of our cars than of ourselves.

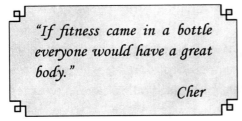

"If fitness came in a bottle everyone would have a great body."

Cher

A recent health and fitness survey showed that only 15% of adults actually have a gym membership. 90% of those stop going to the gym within 90 days of getting their membership.

About half of all adults claim to exercise regularly, either by jogging, walking, attending to a Yoga or Zumba class, or using fitness equipment in the home. For most people, however, getting exercise and staying fit isn't part of their daily routines.

The key to fitness is to find ways to include activity in your lifestyle. There are many simple things you can do every day that will improve your level of fitness. For example, when you go shopping don't park in the space closest to the door. Park far away from the door. You'll get more exercise.

When you go into an office building for a meeting or appointment on a second or third floor, don't take the elevator—walk up. It will give your body a healthy aerobic boost.

The biggest excuse for not staying fit is "not enough time," but there are many easy ways to add fitness to your daily routines.

If you're watching TV don't just sit there. Get some hand weights and do some arm exercises. Stretch out on your sofa and do some leg lifts.

Lay on the carpet and do some situps or crunches. You'll still see your show but you'll tone your body at the same time.

Putting yourself first means making time for exercise and healthy eating. If you are serious about nurturing your personal brand to be in control of your life, take control of your health. Not only will you increase your stamina, you'll look and feel better. You'll also have a positive impact on your wallet. Good health means you're not spending money on prescriptions, doctor visits, and over-the-counter drugs.

My 91-year-old dad keeps an exercise bike in his garage. He rides it every day that he doesn't get enough physical activity from his daily chores and routines. He mows his own lawn, rakes his leaves, cleans his house, and cooks his meals himself. He could easily afford to pay others to do these things for him, but as he says, "Why waste the money? It gives me something to do and keeps me busy." He is in better shape and health than many people who are my age.

Taking care of yourself is also about having a great image. In the world of branding, the quality of the product is not enough to make it a top brand. It also has to have the right packaging and the right look. Lots of money goes into designing the right package, choosing the right colors, and creating the right look.

Being in good health and staying fit contribute to the image you present. But it is only the beginning. Your image communicates powerful messages about you. Just as the packaging of a product is what grabs your attention when you shop, the way you present yourself makes a first impression about you when you meet people. Your packaging includes your clothes and grooming.

In 1975 John Molloy wrote the book *Dress for Success*. It was an instant bestseller. The book used research data about how people respond to different styles of clothing to advise people on their wardrobe choices. What we choose to wear communicates messages about how we see ourselves.

Color is another factor in first impressions. The significance of color is key in product branding. Color palettes affect how different types of people respond to different products. They also affect our moods. A woman in a red dress makes a distinctively different impact than a women in a lavender dress.

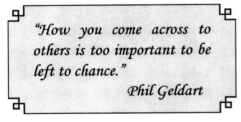

"How you come across to others is too important to be left to chance."

Phil Geldart

In my weekly marketing e-newsletter, Monday Morning Marketing Muse, I've written several articles about the power of color in communication, branding, and image. What colors do you choose to communicate your message? What styles have you selected to communicate what your personal brand is about? What grooming decisions do you make about your physical appearance that are sending image messages to others?

What is your image? Do you have one? If you don't, what do you think it should be?

The final part of taking care of yourself is to have time in your life for tranquility, peace, relaxation, and leisure that keeps you stress-free. There will always be things that happen to you, that you can't prevent, which cause stress. However, if you have control you'll know how to relieve or eliminate the stress.

The statistics on stress are distressing. 80% say that work has a significant impact on their stress. 73% indicate that money is their number one cause of stress. 30% of children say they are stressed about their parents' financial situations. More than 60% of the Millennial Generation say they are stressed. 75% of people report dealing with a highly stressful situation every two weeks.

When you look at those statistics it becomes very clear why you need to follow the steps in *The Success Myth* to get you in control of your life, and living the life you want. Putting yourself first includes taking time to fight stress in your life.

> *"There's never enough time to do all the nothing you want."*
> *Bill Waterson*
> *[Calvin and Hobbes]*

There is not just one way to fight stress. It's different for everyone. What are the stressbusters that work for you? When I think of all the people I know well, and what they do to de-stress, I realize just how long and varied a list of stressbusters can be. Categories include escapes such as going to a movie or reading a book; being in nature at the woods, the mountains, a lake, or the beach; physical and sports activities from golfing to skiing to dancing; time with hobbies; being pampered at a spa; physical challenges such as rock climbing; and much more.

As the final list in creating the life you want, identify the ways you take care of yourself by answering this question:

What do you do to PAMPER yourself, TAKE CARE of yourself, and to KEEP BALANCE in your life?

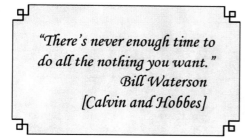

_____

_____

_____

_____

_____

_____

_____

_____

_____

_____

_____

_____

_____

The choices we make in taking care of our health, fitness, image, and stress are part of the balance of having the ideal life. Think about the choices you've made. Which ones are good? Which ones should you change?

These are changes you can make simply by doing something different. They don't require massive actions on your part. Buy healthy foods and eat them in reasonable portions. Add more exercise to your daily routines. You can walk anywhere you want for free. Think about the image you present and what it says about you? What would it take to modify it?

Lastly, think about how much time you spend doing things just for you! Are you putting yourself first?

Look again at what makes you happy. How do the things on that list relate to things you can do to take care of yourself? Can you combine two or more things on your happy list to not only give you a happier life but a healthier one?

If you are among the 80% who have stress from work, what could you do that you love? If you are among the 73% stressed about money, what did you learn from Chapter 8 that can make that stress go away?

Every chapter in this book is about taking care of yourself. When you have good self-esteem about your personal brand, you're ready to take control.

Chapter 13

Create Your Ideal Life

"You miss 100% of the shots you never take."
Wayne Gretzky

Think about what happens in a typical day for you. What are all the ways you compromise in order to accommodate what life throws at you? How many times each day are you being controlled instead of being in control?

Is what happens on TV more thrilling than your own life? Do you dream about escaping your life? Do you look at others and wish for what they have? Are you stuck in a daydream about what you want, what you could be, how you could change, but not doing anything about it?

If you feel your life is fading before your eyes, is never going to start, or you're never going to have the opportunity to have the life you want, get out of that state of mind and make the decision right now to take control of your life.

> *"Don't be trapped by living with the results of other people's thinking."*
> *Steve Jobs*

Look at your score from the quiz in chapter 1. Write your score here, followed by the description of what that score means:

_____

_____

This is your assessment of your life. It shows what level of change you want to create. For some of you it may take only a few small things that will put you in control of your life. For others it might indicate that big changes are ahead for you.

When I started developing this personal branding process I took assessment of my life. My score was 70. I was unhappy with many parts of my life and wanted to change them. When I looked at which questions had the really low numbers circled I knew what parts of my life needed changed.

By using my specific answers to the questions in this book, I identified what I needed to change. That's how it works, and how it will work for you.

Your answers in this book will guide you through your personal SWOT (Strengths, Weaknesses, Opportunities, Threats) analysis that will help you create your successful personal brand. When I do SWOT analysis for companies I always start with the weaknesses because it is essential to eliminate them in order to deal with the other categories.

Your weaknesses are what you identified in Chapter 6 as those things that make you unhappy. What are they? Is there a common theme about what makes you unhappy?

Your first step is to get them out of your life.

I recommend that you get a notebook or set up a computer file for your SWOT process. Do it in a spreadsheet format. A sample SWOT process spreadsheet is shown on pages 122 through 125

SAMPLE: Personal Strategic Plan for the Life You Want

WEAKNESSES	ACTIONS	START	FINISH
(Things that make you unhappy)			

SAMPLE: Personal Strategic Plan for the Life You Want

THREATS	ACTIONS	START	FINISH
(What prevents you from having the life you want?)			

SAMPLE: Personal Strategic Plan for the Life You Want

STRENGTHS	ACTIONS	START	FINISH
(Your personal brand attributes, skills and talents, friends, spouse/signficant other if that applies, and what you do for yourself.)			

SAMPLE: Personal Strategic Plan for the Life You Want

OPPORTUNITIES	ACTIONS	START	FINISH
(What you want your life to be, what makes you happy, and what is important to you.)			

List all of your weaknesses in your first column (the things that make you unhappy.) In your second column write what action(s) you need to take to eliminate each weakness. In your third column write your start date for the action and in your fourth column you will eventually write your completion date—the date when you eliminated this weakness.

Your second page will be your THREATS. These are what you listed in Chapter 5 as the things that prevent you from having the life you want. For each of these you will also need an action column where you write what you need to do about each threat, your start date for doing it, and your completion date when you've achieved success.

> *"If today were the last day of my life, would I want to do what I am about to do today?"*
>
> *Steve Jobs*

In Chapters 4 and 7 you have already created answers that indicate what you will change when you eliminate the threats and weaknesses. They will show you the kind of life you want and help you evaluate what you can do to make the right changes.

Are there common themes in your threats and weaknesses? Statistically the two most common themes would relate to your job and money. Did that happen for you?

If yes, start with your job. Look at your answers from Chapter 7. What do you love? Are you doing what you love? If yes, do you dislike where or how you work right now? If so your options are to find a way to do what you love in a different way or at a different place.

If money is also on your list of threats or weaknesses, look at what you wrote in Chapter 8. Also refer back to the four tips in Chapter 8. There will be several actions you can take so that you make money work for you and have more of it.

Many people think that if they get a raise it will solve their problems. It doesn't. Every time we get more income we increase our lifestyle and use it all up. It's like the government constantly raising taxes because they won't control their spending.

You will need to control and change the way you manage money. Of course you need money for essentials, but Chapter 8 shows you that you may be wasting money without realizing it. You can spend smarter. Always question how spending money will get you closer to the life you want, when you consider a non-essential purchase. If it doesn't, don't spend it.

What if it takes every penny you make just to pay for the essentials, and you feel that you can't use the tips in Chapter 8? Perhaps you are one of the 59% of people who live beyond your means and use credit to fund your lifestyle.

"I went to a bookstore and asked the saleswoman 'Where's the self help section?' She said if she told me it would defeat the purpose."

George Carlin

You will have some major changes to make. And you have no time to waste getting started. First, you need to acknowledge that you need help. In most communities there are many free services that help people plan a course of action when they get in over their heads with financial obligations. If it is very serious for you, consulting with a bankruptcy attorney may be helpful.

Two of the most important lessons in this book are to Put Yourself First and Don't Live Your Life to Impress Others. Don't let worrying about what others think prevent you from taking an action that could make your life better.

After completing all your action points to rid yourself of the Weaknesses and Threats in your strategic plan, focus on your Strengths and Opportunities.

Using the same format, start page 3 of your analysis by listing your STRENGTHS. You've already identified them in Chapter 3 as your brand attributes and Chapter 9 as your skills and talent. Your strengths are your personal brand. They're what make you different, special, and unique from everyone else.

In the action section list things you could do, but aren't doing, to leverage your strengths so they help you get to the life you want.

The second part of your strengths is your list of friends from Chapter 11. Friends form a network that adds strength and stability to your life. Networks help move you forward. They're a resource for the opportunities you want. Are there people in your network who share your interests? They will make your personal brand stronger.

Being around like-minded people is essential to being a successful brand. Businesses use this same principle. It's why when Wendy's puts up a new restaurant they put it near a McDonald's. It's why the cereal aisle at your supermarket is packed with choices. It's why major brands keep coming out with new spinoffs. Those spinoffs get them into new and different market niches of like-minded people.

Now you're ready for page 4, which is your OPPORTUNITES. Start with your list from Chapter 4. What are the things you want your life to be. Write the actions you need to take to make each one happen.

Here's an example: If you wrote "living at the beach" as something you wanted your life to be, your actions would include buying a house at the beach. But to do that you may need to sell your existing house. You may need to think about a new career doing something you love that will sustain your beach lifestyle.

I went to a family reunion last year, and got caught up with aunts, uncles, and cousins from my mother's side of my family I hadn't seen in decades. There was one cousin I especially wanted to see. We were the same age and had done a lot together when we were kids. He had married my best friend, (her first husband), but after their divorce I lost track of him.

It was August, and he wasn't there because he was at the beach. He and another cousin loved fishing at the beach. I learned that they saved some money, quit their jobs, and moved to Rehoboth Beach, Delaware. They bought a boat and the appropriate permits and licenses, and opened a fishing charter business. Now they have multiple boats and employees and spend every day doing exactly what they love. It's a family affair. Their wives run the office end of the business, which they enjoy, while the men spend their days on the water. My cousins made their dreams come true.

> *"A pessimist sees the difficulty in every opportunity. An optimist sees the opportunity in every difficulty."*
> *Winston Churchill*

Turn your opportunities into success for you. Remember my point about how a positive attitude can interfere with action. Don't spend your life thinking that if you are patient, opportunities will come your way. If you do, one day you may find yourself thinking "if only."

Next, add the items on your list of those things that are important to you from Chapter 9. What opportunities are on that list? If you wrote that the plight of abused animals is important to you, what opportunities exist for you to make a difference? What talents do you have that you could use to make a difference in that cause?

Life must have purpose. The writer Robert Byrne said that, "The purpose of life is purpose."

Byrne has lived a colorful life full of many different accomplishments. Now 82, he is an excellent example of how many different talents and interests can be merged together in a life with purpose. His first career path was as a civil engineer. But he loved to write. So he combined both and wrote for *Western Construction* magazine. In 1961 he became the editor, a job he did for ten years.

During this time he also wrote novels. In 1977 he became a full-time novelist. He enjoyed playing billiards and wrote seven books about the subject including the now classic *Byrne's Standard Book of Pool and Billiards*, considered to be one of the definitive books on the subject. He's received numerous awards for writing and billiards.

His first wife was the daughter of the violinist Jascha Heifetz. His second wife was an artist, and because of those associations he supports the arts as part of his purpose. He was a tournament chess player and an amateur magician who published tricks in *Genie* magazine. Byrne always used his writing to share his talent and knowledge with others.

The combination of his interests, talents, and accomplishments can't be categorized. He is a great example of how each of us is unique and how each of us can create a varied world of opportunity to use our talents and interests to have purpose in our lives.

Now that you have your four SWOT sheets finished, be sure your time tables don't overwhelm you and defeat the purpose of taking control.

Allow plenty of time to do those things you identified in Chapter 12 that keep you healthy and stress-free.

If, as discussed in Chapter 10, you are still looking for the perfect relationship, finding it is your greatest opportunity. I believe that finding the right person to share your life adds more dimension to your success and happiness than anything else. In that chapter I shared my process for how to know when you've found the right person for you. You, however, need to take the actions to meet people.

I believe the best way to meet the person who is right for you is to put yourself in situations with like-minded people as often as possible. Attend events, join clubs or organizations, network with others, accept introductions from family and friends, and go on dates (as many as possible.) Sure, you might have a lot of bad dates, but consider it practice that helps you recognize the "real thing" when it comes along.

You'll meet a lot of people who are already in relationships. The statistics show that many of those are not good relationships. You may find that your perfect match exists in an imperfect relationship with someone else. It will be more complicated, but life is too short to stay in a bad relationship. Find the way to end a bad relationship so you are free to be in the right one.

In the spring of 2009 I went to a resort in Tennessee with the man who became my perfect relationship. It was our first trip together. The resort was for people who owned and showed horses. There were trail rides, shows, cookouts, dancing, and lots of fun that was totally new to me. I had never been on a horse in my life! There were five other couples we joined up with, all friends of his I had never met.

On the first evening a bunch of us were sitting around having drinks and talking, and I learned that one of the couples had wanted to be high school sweethearts in the Louisiana town where they lived. But he was a few years older than her and her daddy wouldn't let her date him. Eventually their lives took different paths. They each married someone else and had families. But neither of them forgot the other and that wistful feeling of the love of youth stayed buried deep within them.

Many years later they both returned to that town for a celebration event and ran into each other. That teenage crush was very much alive. They were older now. Their children were grown and living their own lives. They decided not to waste another year without each other. They took the actions needed to take advantage of the opportunity missed so many years before, and created a new life together.

Start now to create your ideal life by implementing the actions recorded in your personal branding SWOT analysis. It may look overwhelming. But you already know the consequences of doing nothing.

Forget the past. You can't change it. But you can use what you learned from it. Start today to create the future you want.

In my last chapter I'll share my story with you of what I did and how this process worked for me. My actions may give you ideas for what your actions should be. The way the process helped me achieve my true success and happiness may give you the encouragement you need to start working on your own.

Take control. Decide you're going to do it. Then get started.

Chapter 14

How it Worked for Me

"If you refuse to accept anything but the very best,
you often get it."

W. Somerset Maugham

I always wanted a career. I wanted it to be a career in journalism. Instead, it became a career in advertising and marketing, but nonetheless, I loved what I did. My first job was for a special interest magazine publishing company located in Pennsylvania. It was a dream job. In the 13 years I worked there I was promoted four times. At the age of 27 I was selected for the management training program. I was 22 when I was hired, and 35 when I left.

By the time I left I was in charge of the advertising and marketing for thirteen different magazines, a travel division that offered both domestic and international trips and tours, and the public relations for the corporation. I was part of the mergers and acquisitions team for expansion. I also had access to a company-owned apartment in Manhattan where I lived when I had work to do in New York City. When I had to fly on company business it was usually in a private plane. Not bad for only being 35.

I walked away from this dream job because when I was 32 I became a mom. Despite all my career accomplishments, nothing could compare to the day my son was born. The day we came home from the hospital my dad and stepmother came to see their new grandson. I have a photo of my dad, me, and the baby. My dad and I both have the biggest, silliest looking grins on our faces. It's one of my favorite pictures.

I took three months of maternity leave to stay home. By the end of the second month I started thinking of ways I could freelance from home and not go back to work. But like so many of us, I just thought about it. I dreamed about it. And I did nothing about it. When I finally went back to work I no longer loved my dream job. I no longer looked forward to the time in Manhattan or the trips in the private plane. I didn't want to leave my son.

It soon became apparent to the people I worked with that I returned a different person than the woman who left a week before her son was born. It wasn't working out. So eventually I looked for a job that wouldn't be as demanding and I found one. It was a perfect fit for me. It was closer to where I lived so my commute was shorter, and there was a church-run day care/preschool for my son only a few blocks from my new office.

The owner of the company was a sweetheart when it came to understanding my priorities as a mom. My son was now three and we enjoyed commuting together. It was OK if I brought him to the office with me when I needed to. It was also OK for me to work at home occasionally when I needed to. I only had to travel once a year that required an overnight absence.

I was already working on my plan on how to do my job from home when my son started kindergarten. I could go to the office while he was at school, then be back home to work from home when he wasn't. But my husband changed my dreams.

Just after our son turned five, he told me he was having problems at work. The company he had worked at for more than 20 years had closed, and he had taken a job at a new company. He had been in his new job for about a year. The following week he decided he was going to quit his new job.

At the age of 37 I was suddenly thrust into the role of being the sole income for our household. And it happened at a time when I was developing a plan to spend more of my time at home. During the next five months my husband had three job offers from new companies, all of them good offers. He turned each one down. He always found something he didn't like about each offer.

I finally realized that he liked not working and he had no intention of ever taking another job. The flexibility I needed to change my life to be home with my son before and after his school hours had vanished.

It also became apparent that my husband wasn't interested in taking advantage of his time to develop a really great bond with his son. If that had happened things might have been OK. When I was home in the evenings and on weekends I tried to make up for the ever-growing distance between my husband and son. The burden of trying to be a supermom, juggling motherhood and career, made me closer to my son but drove me away from my husband.

This situation continued because I allowed it to continue. That was my first big mistake. I changed jobs in 1988 and again in 1992. In 1996 I bought out the company I worked for and became the owner of my own advertising/marketing agency. The more money I earned, the bigger the lifestyle my husband wanted to live. Business was good. In 1997 we moved to be nearer my business and my son's high school.

We moved into a house I didn't want. But my husband had his heart set on it. I knew it was too expensive and I would need to work even harder. Of course he didn't care about that. He didn't work. Once again I had allowed something to happen to me that wasn't what I wanted.

> *"The average man is a conformist, accepting miseries and disasters with the stoicism of a cow standing in the rain."*
>
> *Colin Wilson*

My business continued to grow and although money wasn't a problem, as all business owners know, you have to plan for the possible threats. My biggest threat was my husband. If the bank account was healthy he found ways to spend it.

In September of 2001 the bottom fell out of my world. On September 11th the world trade towers in NYC, the Pentagon, and a plane were all hit by terrorists. The fallout from that tragedy created mini disasters throughout the country. In my industry,118,000 people lost jobs within 10 months. Advertising businesses went out of business. Consumer spending dried up. Companies stopped advertising while they waited for the aftermath to settle.

For several months I had little or no revenue coming in. In September of 2001 my son entered his freshman year of college. At the same time my revenue stream dried up I had significant college tuition payments to make on top of all the other ongoing expenses for my business and my home. And my husband still didn't work.

For the first time in my life, at the age of 50, I needed credit. Fortunately I had it. I had a line of credit for my company that I used to keep people on payroll as long as possible. By the time I realized I needed to let them go, I had gotten into deep debt that I couldn't repay.

I should have put myself first. If I had I would have not used so much credit trying to save everyone else. Three months after the World Trade Centers were hit I took a part-time job working two evenings a week and every weekend. I was now working full time trying to keep my business going and part-time to make as much extra money as possible. I was working about 90 hours each week. My husband continued to not work.

I had been living well before this happened so I had things I could sell. My son's tuition for his second semester that year was paid for by selling the sports car I had bought as a fun indulgence. Actually I didn't drive it. My husband did. I sold the baby grand piano. I did everything possible to generate income. And my husband continued to not work. I finally decided I wouldn't tolerate it any more and insisted that he do something to help out. He got a part-time job that paid low wages, opened his own bank account, and put his earnings in his account.

My son graduated from college with several job offers. He took the one he liked best, and lived at home for few months to build up a nest egg before moving into his own place in 2006. When he moved out my husband and I separated. At first we just lived apart in the same house.

This was when I started working on adapting my strategic planning processes to create my ideal life. Here is what I did, how it worked, and the results I have today.

My first decision was that from now on I would put myself first. My first step was to free myself from my spouse and the financial burdens of our house.

I asked him to move out of the house. I sold the house. The house was in both our names, so we split the profit 50/50.

I then downsized my life to an apartment that I loved. My cost of living was now greatly reduced. My business had bounced back and was doing well, but it was still taking more of my time than I wanted.

> *"There is only one thing that makes a dream impossible to achieve: the fear of failure."*
> *Paulo Coelho*

By eliminating two of my obstacles, however, I had more money and more freedom. I looked at what I wanted my life to be. The big dream was the one I told you about in Chapter 5. In the fall of 2008 I went to France and by being there I realized the dream was better than the reality. When I came back I crossed it off the list of what I wanted my life to be.

Within a week of getting back from France my husband changed my dreams again.

I received a notice he was suing me for spousal support and more. I hadn't done anything about filing for a divorce. Being separated had been enough. I wasn't looking for a new husband so a divorce didn't seem important at the time. When I read the summons to attend the hearing I realized I was still letting my positive attitude that everything would work out, prevent me from taking actions that put me in control. I had lost control again.

I will spare you the rancor and viciousness of everything that happened in the divorce and will sum it up by saying that by the time my divorce was final I held, and still hold, a firm belief that the justice and legal systems in this country are a sham. I hadn't expected it. This was my second marriage. My first divorce was amicable.

The result was that this self-serving man, who had mooched off of me most of his adult life, was entitled to everything I had because I had the earning potential to make more and he didn't. The divorce left me with $239 in the bank.

During my divorce I commiserated with many female friends who had been through experiences similar to mine. One friend had an ex who, while they were married, gambled them into financial ruin. He had built up immense gambling debts. In her divorce she was saddled with the responsibility of paying all his debts, paying him support, and paying for gambling addiction counseling for him after the divorce.

I also talked with many men who were treated the same way by greedy, vindictive ex-wives. The reality is that if you are successful, in a divorce you are punished for your success. It is not about gender; it's about who is the most successful. It's a form of socialism where those who work hard get the results of their hard work taken from them and given to those who want everything provided for them without having to do anything to earn it.

I closed my business in order to get divorced. My ex had gotten my share of the proceeds of the house I paid for, my savings, and I had to continue to pay spousal support that had been awarded prior to the divorce. On top of that, I was responsible for all the debts that were still owed from our marriage plus those from my business.

For a year I struggled to turn my life around financially. By August of 2010 I realized I was drowning in financial obligations I couldn't meet. I started credit negotiations and was successful at getting some obligations reduced and paid off. In 2009 I had moved to a smaller, less costly apartment so I had downsized my living as much as I was willing to.

In 2011 I met with a bankruptcy attorney. Both my divorce attorney and my business attorney had recommended that I pursue bankruptcy back in 2009 but I didn't take their advice. I should have. But once again I did not put myself first. I felt that I needed to do everything possible to repay debts, even if it meant not doing anything for myself.

The bankruptcy attorney was wonderful. She put things into perspective for me when she asked me, "Carol, the system has screwed you. How long are you going to let it get away with that?" She was right. My bankruptcy was approved and awarded in 2012.

I have not mentioned the most important and significant change in my life. I didn't go through all of this alone. Without the fabulous new person who came into my life I may not have gotten through it.

In Chapter 10 I told you I had found my perfect relationship. We met by having a mutual friend. (Networking is a great way to meet new people!) We first met by phone in December of 2008. Our first date followed two weeks later. We both lived in Pennsylvania, but in different parts of the state. It was a four-hour drive one way.

By the time we had our first date I was in the midst of the nasty divorce and court proceedings. We commiserated. In the 1990s he had gone through the same process, although his was much nastier than mine, and his children were still under 18 at the time. But the parallels in our situations were amazing. We both had spouses who didn't want to work, loved to spend money so we had to keep working harder and harder, and then played the "earning power" card during the divorce to get all the assets.

He knew my pain. He had been through it. He understood the depths of despair it can take you to and he knew from experience that the "justice system," when it comes to divorce, is an oxymoron.

It was fitting that on July 3rd, 2009, he arrived at my apartment to spend the July 4th holiday weekend together. He came in and handed me my mail that I hadn't yet collected, and in that mail was the divorce decree. We celebrated! I truly did have independence. Now we could get on with building our new life together.

In the spring of 2010 we became engaged, just two days before my stepmother died. We had been up to visit my parents three days before she died and had gone out to dinner with them. As we left their house my stepmother pulled me close and said softly to me, "Carol, I really like Dan. He's a keeper." They were the last words she ever said to me. Three days later she was gone, and I hadn't yet called to tell her about getting engaged.

My fiancé had financially recovered from his divorce, which had been finalized years before mine even started. He knew I was struggling and offered financial help, which I turned down for as long as possible. By August 2010 I could no longer turn it down. For a year, from August 2010 to October 2011, while I struggled to deal with my debts, he made sure I didn't hit rock bottom the way he had. He provided money when I needed it, and he provided support, understanding, hope, and love all the time.

We worked on plans to create our new life. I couldn't and wouldn't do anything legally, such as marriage, while I had obligations to fulfill. I didn't want my burdens to become his. Now that I am once again in control of my life we have plans for what happily ever after will be for us.

If I hadn't finally taken action to get out of my old life, I would never have met this amazing man. My happiness doesn't depend on him, but because of him I have more of it than I ever imagined was possible.

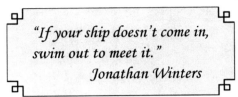

"If your ship doesn't come in, swim out to meet it."

Jonathan Winters

Another part of the strategic plan was my career. When I closed my agency I had discussed a business arrangement with a very good professional friend. I moved my work for my clients into his business. We had a financial agreement that made this appealing for both of us. I stayed with that agreement for two years, from the summer of 2009 to the summer of 2011.

Those were challenging years in the American economy. 2009 was the worst hit year of the recession. 2010 wasn't much better. Our merger helped us both. We still remain friends and I still try to send business his way when I can.

By June of 2011 I decided I wanted more time to try to spend with my fiancé. We were alternating weekends of driving the four-hour trip.

We decided to take the month of July off and spend it together. It was a fabulous month. We traveled through 16 states. When we got back I set up an office in my home to provide services for my marketing clients. I also set up an office at his house so I could work from there. It opened a new dimension to our relationship and gave us more flexibility for being together.

Today we live a lifestyle where we spend as much time together as possible. Neither of us is retired, so we each have businesses to maintain. But we're making plans. The picture of "what I want my life to be," that I first created back in 2006, is very different today. I could never have imagined it being this good when I started working on my new life seven years ago.

In putting myself first I haven't abandoned having purpose in my life. I was raised with the examples of giving back and doing things to help others. My parents and my grandparents were great role models.

Since 2008 I have been a mentor for SCORE. If you don't know, SCORE is a national organization of successful business people who volunteer their time to help entrepreneurs and business owners. There are 364 chapters across the U.S. Collectively those chapters have 13,000 volunteers who help others for nothing more than the satisfaction of giving back.

In my local chapter I volunteer with 64 others. I have met many exceptional men and women through my association with SCORE, in the volunteers I work with and the business owners and entrepreneurs we advise. My local chapter, in Lancaster, PA, was just selected as the Chapter of the Year for 2013 in recognition of the quality we deliver.

The satisfaction I get from being part of this organization is another part of what I want my life to be. If I hadn't put myself first, I would not have had the time or means to be a SCORE mentor and have this purpose in my life.

> *"Success is liking yourself, liking what you do, and liking how you do it."*
> *Maya Angelou*

I hope that reading how I made changes in my life by following the process described in my book will help you think about how to make the changes you want.

I've seriously changed the size of my life. I've simplified it in order to have happiness. My quiz score from chapter one is now 131 instead of

70. I've changed a lot, but there are still some things to improve. I keep taking actions to get all of my answers to 10.

It's your turn. Look at all the questions in the quiz that you couldn't answer with a 10. Use the process to turn all your answers into 10s. The life you want is within your reach. You may have to stretch a little to reach it. It may not always be easy. Your path to personal success may take you on some detours, but with your plan you'll always find your way back.

> You have brains in your head
> You have feet in your shoes
> You can steer yourself
> Any direction you choose
> You're on your own
> And you know what you know
> And YOU are the guy who'll decide where to go.

> Dr. Seuss

INDEX

A

B

C

D

M

N

O

P

Q

R

V

W

Y

Author's Message to You

 Thank you for reading *The Success Myth*. Are you now ready to reinvent yourself and your life?

If yes, you don't have to go through this process alone.

There are many ways you can continue to get the encouragement, support, and direction you need to eliminate all the "if only" aspects of your life and make your dreams come true.

Go to my website, www.carolguild.com, and you can . . .

- Get free downloads of additional information
- Sign up for my free bi-weekly E-newsletter
- Let me know if you're interested in listening in on one of my free motivational teleseminars
- Get information about my regional workshops and two-day retreats

Don't lose the momentum and motivation for changing your life.

Live Happy!

CPSIA information can be obtained at www.ICGtesting.com
Printed in the USA
BVOW03s1921300914

368924BV00002B/27/P